SELF-LEARNING MANAGEMENT SERIES

VIBRANT
PUBLISHERS

BUSINESS STATISTICS ESSENTIALS

YOU ALWAYS WANTED TO KNOW

Transforming statistical data into actionable
insights for business success

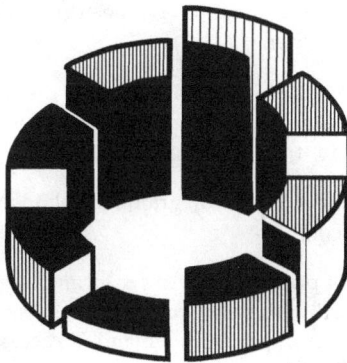

BIANCA SZASZ, Ph.D.

BUSINESS STATISTICS ESSENTIALS YOU ALWAYS WANTED TO KNOW

First Edition

Published by Vibrant Publishers LLC, USA, www.vibrantpublishers.com

Paperback ISBN 13: 978-1-63651-482-6
Ebook ISBN 13: 978-1-63651-483-3
Hardback ISBN 13: 978-1-63651-484-0

Library of Congress Control Number: 2025935453

This publication is designed to provide accurate and authoritative information in regard to the subject matter covered. The Author has made every effort in the preparation of this book to ensure the accuracy of the information. However, information in this book is sold without warranty either expressed or implied. The Author or the Publisher will not be liable for any damages caused or alleged to be caused either directly or indirectly by this book.

All trademarks and registered trademarks mentioned in this publication are the property of their respective owners. These trademarks are used for editorial and educational purposes only, without intent to infringe upon any trademark rights. This publication is independent and has not been authorized, endorsed, or approved by any trademark owner.

Vibrant Publishers' books are available at special quantity discount for sales promotions, or for use in corporate training programs. For more information please write to bulkorders@vibrantpublishers.com

Please email feedback / corrections (technical, grammatical or spelling) to spellerrors@vibrantpublishers.com

Vibrant publishes in a variety of print and electronic formats and by print-on-demand. Some material included with standard print versions of this book may not be included in e-books or in print-on-demand. To access the complete catalogue of Vibrant Publishers, visit www.vibrantpublishers.com

3. **Request the resources:** Scroll down to the "Request Sample Book/ Online Resource" section.

4. **Enter your details:** Enter your preferred email ID and select "Online Resource" as the resource type. Lastly, select "user type" and submit the request.

5. **Check your inbox:** The resources will be delivered directly to your email.

Alternatively, for quick access, simply scan the QR code below to go directly to the product page and request the online resources by filling in the required details.

bit.ly/bs-slm

Happy learning!

Exclusive Online Resources for You

As our valued reader, your purchase of this book includes access to exclusive online resources designed to enhance your learning experience. These resources can be downloaded from our website, www.vibrantpublishers.com, and are created to help you apply Business Statistics concepts effectively.

Online resources for this book include the following three essential components:

1. Discrete Probability Distributions Template
2. Data Presentation (Charts & Graphs) in Excel
3. Solutions Guide to Key Quiz Questions

Why are these online resources valuable?

- **Hands-on practice:** These ready-to-use templates guide you to apply concepts directly and reinforce real-world skills.

- **Visual learning:** They help you learn data presentation techniques with practical Excel charts and graphs to better interpret statistical insights.

- **Concept clarity:** They deepen your understanding with guided solutions to key quiz questions, helping solidify learning and boost confidence.

How to access your online resources:

1. **Visit the website:** Go to www.vibrantpublishers.com
2. **Find your book:** Navigate to the book's product page via the "Shop" menu or by searching for the book title in the search bar.

SELF-LEARNING MANAGEMENT SERIES

TITLE	PAPERBACK* ISBN

BUSINESS AND ENTREPRENEURSHIP

BUSINESS COMMUNICATION ESSENTIALS	9781636511634
BUSINESS ETHICS ESSENTIALS	9781636513324
BUSINESS LAW ESSENTIALS	9781636511702
BUSINESS PLAN ESSENTIALS	9781636511214
BUSINESS STRATEGY ESSENTIALS	9781949395778
ENTREPRENEURSHIP ESSENTIALS	9781636511603
INTERNATIONAL BUSINESS ESSENTIALS	9781636513294
PRINCIPLES OF MANAGEMENT ESSENTIALS	9781636511542

COMPUTER SCIENCE AND TECHNOLOGY

BLOCKCHAIN ESSENTIALS	9781636513003
CYBERSECURITY ESSENTIALS	9781636514888
MACHINE LEARNING ESSENTIALS	9781636513775
PYTHON ESSENTIALS	9781636512938

DATA SCIENCE FOR BUSINESS

BUSINESS ANALYTICS ESSENTIALS	9781636514154
BUSINESS INTELLIGENCE ESSENTIALS	9781636513362
DATA ANALYTICS ESSENTIALS	9781636511184

FINANCIAL LITERACY AND ECONOMICS

COST ACCOUNTING & MANAGEMENT ESSENTIALS	9781636511030
FINANCIAL ACCOUNTING ESSENTIALS	9781636510972
FINANCIAL MANAGEMENT ESSENTIALS	9781636511009
MACROECONOMICS ESSENTIALS	9781636511818
MICROECONOMICS ESSENTIALS	9781636511153
PERSONAL FINANCE ESSENTIALS	9781636511849
PRINCIPLES OF ECONOMICS ESSENTIALS	9781636512334

*Also available in Hardback & Ebook formats

SELF-LEARNING MANAGEMENT SERIES

TITLE	PAPERBACK* ISBN

HR, DIVERSITY, AND ORGANIZATIONAL SUCCESS

DIVERSITY, EQUITY, AND INCLUSION ESSENTIALS	9781636512976
DIVERSITY IN THE WORKPLACE ESSENTIALS	9781636511122
HR ANALYTICS ESSENTIALS	9781636510347
HUMAN RESOURCE MANAGEMENT ESSENTIALS	9781949395839
ORGANIZATIONAL BEHAVIOR ESSENTIALS	9781636512303
ORGANIZATIONAL DEVELOPMENT ESSENTIALS	9781636511481

LEADERSHIP AND PERSONAL DEVELOPMENT

DECISION MAKING ESSENTIALS	9781636510026
INCLUSIVE LEADERSHIP ESSENTIALS	9781636514765
INDIA'S ROAD TO TRANSFORMATION: WHY LEADERSHIP MATTERS	9781636512273
LEADERSHIP ESSENTIALS	9781636510316
TIME MANAGEMENT ESSENTIALS	9781636511665

MODERN MARKETING AND SALES

CONSUMER BEHAVIOR ESSENTIALS	9781636513263
DIGITAL MARKETING ESSENTIALS	9781949395747
MARKETING MANAGEMENT ESSENTIALS	9781636511788
MARKET RESEARCH ESSENTIALS	9781636513744
MODERN ADVERTISING ESSENTIALS	9781636514857
SALES MANAGEMENT ESSENTIALS	9781636510743
SERVICES MARKETING ESSENTIALS	9781636511733
SOCIAL MEDIA MARKETING ESSENTIALS	9781636512181

*Also available in Hardback & Ebook formats

SELF-LEARNING MANAGEMENT SERIES

TITLE	PAPERBACK* ISBN

OPERATIONS MANAGEMENT

AGILE ESSENTIALS	9781636510057
OPERATIONS & SUPPLY CHAIN MANAGEMENT ESSENTIALS	9781949395242
PRODUCT MANAGEMENT ESSENTIALS	9781636514796
PROJECT MANAGEMENT ESSENTIALS	9781636510712
STAKEHOLDER ENGAGEMENT ESSENTIALS	9781636511511

CURRENT AFFAIRS

DIGITAL SHOCK	9781636513805

*Also available in Hardback & Ebook formats

About the Author

Bianca Szasz, Ph.D., is a highly accomplished space systems engineer with a strong foundation in data analysis, statistical modeling, and quantitative research. Her work on complex satellite systems has involved rigorous application of statistical tools for environmental testing and thermal analysis. She earned her Ph.D. in Space Engineering from the Kyushu Institute of Technology, Japan, through the prestigious United Nations/ Japan Long-term Fellowship Programme (Post-graduate Study on Nano-Satellite Technologies – PNST).

Her career spans multiple international organizations across the UAE, Japan, the USA, Germany, Hungary, the Czech Republic, and Romania, where she has contributed to different aerospace projects. Currently serving as a Senior Engineer – Mission Assurance in the UAE, she ensures the reliability and safety of advanced space systems. Her previous roles include space systems engineer, senior mission design and trajectory engineer, aerospace research engineer, and assistant professor, reflecting her deep technical knowledge and leadership in space engineering. She has also collaborated with top research institutions, including the German Aerospace Center (DLR) in Germany and Nagoya University in Japan.

As an advocate for global collaboration in space research, she serves as the point of contact for the University Space Engineering Consortium (UNISEC-Global) in Romania, fostering international partnerships in space technology.

Beyond her engineering career, Bianca has a strong analytical and strategic mindset, which has led her to pursue an MBA to bridge the gap between technology and business strategy. Her passion for data analytics, decision-making, and strategic planning naturally aligns with the principles of business statistics, a field critical to informed leadership and operational success.

With her diverse experience in technical and managerial domains, Bianca stands at the intersection of engineering, research, and business, offering invaluable insights to professionals and leaders alike.

What Experts Say About This Book!

Business Statistics Essentials delivers what it promises: It provides fundamental statistical knowledge that is specifically designed for business applications. The book's value is derived from its harmonious integration of both theory and practice. For instance, the chapters on Descriptive Statistics and Probability Distributions helped me not only understand the concepts but also apply them to real business scenarios. The structure of the book is learner-friendly, with summaries, further reading suggestions, and self-assessment tests at the end of each chapter, and the tone is engaging.

**– Sara Szasz, Chief Executive Officer,
Previ SRL**

Business Statistics Essentials is one of the most practical and well-organized guides I have ever encountered on the subject. The book simplifies complex concepts into easy-to-understand lessons, starting with the fundamentals in Chapter 1 and concluding with hypothesis testing in Chapter 9.

**– Tamer Aburouk, Senior Satellite EPS Engineer,
Space42**

A lot of concepts are considered "math" and avoided by anybody who wasn't very keen on mathematics during their school years. Yet you need these concepts to understand even a COVID statistic, and without them, you would be wandering through a forest in the dark if you're in any management position. Bianca's book is practical and fun, with plenty of examples and exercises to help you use these concepts outside the math class and into real-world scenarios.

**– Catalin Puiu, Executive Director,
Electro-Total**

What Experts Say About This Book!

Business Statistics Essentials by Bianca Szasz is a well-written and practical guide that makes learning statistics much easier and more approachable. The book covers a wide range of topics, from basic data collection and descriptive statistics to more advanced areas like probability, regression, hypothesis testing, and even using statistics in marketing and inventory management.

What I liked most is how clearly the concepts are explained. Even if you don't have a strong background in statistics, the book guides you step by step in a very understandable way. I also really appreciated the thoughtful use of visuals like charts, tables, and plots, which really help make the content easier to follow. Plus, each chapter ends with practice questions (with answers!) so you can test your understanding right away.

The book is a great resource whether you're a student, a beginner in business, or someone who just wants to build confidence in using data to make smarter decisions.

Happy reading! Hope you find it as helpful and engaging as I did!

– Elena Marin, QA Manager

Table of Contents

Acknowledgments

A blend of professional dedication and personal inspiration led me to write this book on Business Statistics. Although my work as a professional in space systems engineering has taken me across the globe, this project has shown me that even in a very technical subject like statistics, the power of clarity, simplicity, and personal connection can make a difference.

The team from Vibrant Publishers was there for me every step of the way, and I am eternally grateful to them. Their passion and professionalism made this journey not only possible but truly enjoyable.

A very special thank you goes to my mother, my sister, and my nephew David, who are back home in Romania. Though miles separate us, with me living and working in the UAE, your love travels with me every day. You have always been there for me, providing unwavering support, stability, and encouragement.

I hope that this book is an educational tool and a reminder to all who read it that there is a story—and people—behind every statistic.

Preface

When the term "Statistics" is mentioned to colleagues or students, there is often a familiar look—a brief moment of confusion or apprehension, quickly followed by a change of topic to something more "exciting." To be honest, I get it. Many years ago, I might have been in the same position, thinking statistics was just a maze of numbers and formulas. Like many, I didn't realize the power behind these numbers and how they could be important for fields such as business. I used to think of statistics as an abstract subject, something you merely had to get through in school. But then, during my time working in research, it all clicked.

My background in statistics has increased my appreciation for the transformative power of statistical analyses in driving business success. As an experienced researcher, I have seen firsthand how statistical techniques, principles, and concepts revolutionize business strategies, optimize processes, and reveal valuable insights.

Newer technological tools such as Customer Relationship Management (CRM) systems, Enterprise Resource Planning (ERP) systems, web and mobile applications analytics, social media networks, and Human Resources (HR) systems continue to generate huge volumes of data for businesses. This has made data-driven decision-making a necessity for businesses.

This understanding led me to write *Business Statistics Essentials You Always Wanted to Know* (*Business Statistics Essentials*) to provide a comprehensive yet practical guide for people in business who want to leverage the power of their business-generated data. *Business Statistics Essentials* is also intended for professionals looking to navigate the world of statistics confidently. It breaks down complex statistical theories and demonstrates how they apply in the business landscape. It uses easy-to-follow steps and clear explanations to solve practical business problems, supported by charts and graphs to enhance comprehension.

I hope this book serves as a valuable resource in your quest to harness the power of data and drive your business forward.

Introduction to the Book

Welcome to the world of Business Statistics—a discipline that transforms raw data into actionable insights. As decision-making evolves, the reliance on intuition or traditional methods of choosing the most logical or seemingly sensible alternative is no longer sufficient in today's complex landscape. The business world has not been spared from this transformation either.

Modern challenges demand solutions rooted in rigorous analysis, and this is where statistics in business becomes indispensable. By providing the tools to analyze trends, uncover patterns, and make informed decisions, statistics has become a cornerstone of success in every industry.

In designing *Business Statistics Essentials*, we have considered all kinds of readers that may interact with the book, whether one has advanced knowledge of statistics or little to no knowledge. This book will equip you with a solid foundation in statistical principles and their practicality in the world of business. The book's content starts with the basics and progresses to advanced topics. But don't let the word 'advanced' scare you—we've ensured every section is as approachable as the first.

What This Book Is About

The book delves into key areas of business statistics, starting with the fundamentals and progressing to more complex topics. It offers a step-by-step journey through statistical techniques, emphasizing their relevance in solving business problems. Each chapter introduces a specific statistical concept, breaks it down into digestible components, and concludes with practical applications to reinforce learning.

What You Can Expect to Learn

You'll gain practical skills in business statistics and insights into key concepts—outlined below—to make informed decisions:

- **A strong foundation**
  The book's introduction provides a brief overview of business statistics, discussing its significance, practical uses, and potential misuse. This lays a foundation for learning statistical concepts and techniques, covered later in the book, in depth.

- **Data mastery**
  You will be familiarized with techniques used to collect data, how to measure and classify data, and how to present the collected data to your audience or stakeholders. You will also understand ethical considerations during the collection of data.

- **Descriptive and inferential statistics**
  You will gain insight into measures of central tendency, variability, and how they summarize and describe data distributions. You will also be led through the selection of samples for studies, while the gist of the book combines all the concepts put together from Chapters One to Eight to test hypotheses about populations.

- **Probability and its applications**
  Understand the principles of probability, from basic rules to advanced distributions, and learn how to combine probability with counting techniques for practical problem-solving.

- **Advanced analytical techniques**
  Dive into correlation and regression analysis to uncover relationships between variables and predict future trends.

- **Decision-making tools**
  Master hypothesis testing and statistical estimation
  to evaluate business scenarios and support decision-
  making under uncertainty.

- **Active learning**
  By helping readers work through practice questions,
  this book promotes active learning. It enables readers
  to apply business statistics topics directly rather than
  just reading about them.

Why This Book Is Unique

Unlike traditional textbooks, *Business Statistics Essentials*
blends theoretical concepts with practical business
applications. Throughout its chapters, you will find:

- **Clear explanations:** Complex statistical concepts
  are simplified without losing depth, making them
  accessible to learners of all backgrounds.

- **Practical examples:** Each topic is accompanied by
  examples that mirror challenges faced in business,
  ensuring relevance and practicality.

- **Engaging visuals:** Data is presented in tables, charts,
  and plots, where necessary, in a clear and visually
  appealing format to help you understand the content
  and questions in the book.

- **Practice questions:** Each chapter ends with practice
  questions. Answers to all questions are also provided to
  help you remember what you learnt in the chapter.

This book promises to take you from whatever level
of knowledge you are at to a skilled level. It will leave
you with the confidence to use statistical concepts and
data to solve business challenges. The book does not

discriminate—whether you desire to advance in your career, grow your business, or excel in academics, this book is your mate to walk with you through that journey.

So let's get started!

Who Can Benefit From This Book?

The design of this book and the approach taken to present the content makes it fit for people from all fields, specifically:

- Anyone who is curious about statistics and its applications in the business environment.
- Professionals in business who want to improve their statistical and data analysis knowledge for accurate decision-making.
- Entrepreneurs and leaders who rely on data to identify new business ventures or opportunities.

No matter your background or goals, this book offers a friendly, step-by-step approach to mastering the essentials of business statistics.

How to Use This Book?

When writing the book, we had in mind the challenges novice readers may likely encounter in their journey of learning business statistics. That is why we structured the book beginning with simpler concepts.

We encourage all readers with scant statistical knowledge in business statistics to begin with the introduction and move sequentially. As a general guide to navigating and utilizing the content effectively, follow these recommendations:

1. **Start at your Level**
   You are free to start with areas that you think are new or where you lack understanding. However, starting with introductory chapters will help you build a strong foundation before tackling more advanced topics.

2. **Focus on specific topics**
   If you are looking to enhance a particular skill, such as probability or hypothesis testing, feel free to jump directly to the relevant chapters. Each chapter is self-contained and provides detailed explanations and examples.

3. **Combine with real-world scenarios**
   As you read, think about how the statistical concepts apply to your work, studies, or business decisions. Relating the material to your experiences will deepen your learning.

4. **Leverage visual aids**
   Pay attention to the diagrams, charts, and scatter plots provided in the chapters. These visuals are included to enhance comprehension and illustrate key points.

5. **Review key takeaways**
   At the end of each chapter we conclude with a summary of key points. Use these summaries to recap your learning.

CHAPTER 1

Introduction to Business Statistics

Key Learning Objectives

- Understand the background and definition of business statistics.
- Explore the applications and importance of business statistics.
- Learn essential terms in statistics.
- Briefly understand the misuse of statistics.

In this chapter, we lay the groundwork that we build upon as we progress through the book. Let's begin by gaining insight into the background of business statistics.

1.1 Background to Business Statistics

Data has emerged as a key component in the ever-changing business world to steer organizations to greater potential. With advancements in technology and unparalleled connectivity in business, organizations have found themselves with vast amounts of data generated from transactions. With this, the billion-dollar question is how to utilize this data for maximum profitability. It is not enough to merely have access to massive volumes of data. The real advantage is applying advanced statistical techniques to draw insights for informed decision-making in business.

Raw data in itself has enormous potential benefits for organizations. With this data, organizations can understand market dynamics, competition, customer behavior, and preferences. However, being able to turn data into a meaningful sense is the real deal. This is the art of business statistics: gathering, evaluating, presenting, and organizing business-related data that supports decision-making in the business environment. Business statistics is especially beneficial to organizations that employ the services of skilled statisticians and data analysts. These professionals analyze vast volumes of raw data and generate insights that could inform policy or decision-making. Decisions backed with data provide stakeholders the confidence to navigate the business landscape.

Thus, making strategic, effective business choices is based on transforming unprocessed data into useful insights. Business statistics accelerates this transformative process, from data to strategy, and allows firms to extract real value from the data at their disposal. This creates true value for them and becomes the cornerstone of tremendous success. Organizations that want to stay ahead of the competition and increase their market relevance must gain an understanding of the business environment along with a proficiency in implementing statistical techniques.

1.2 Applications of Business Statistics

Business statistics plays a crucial role in decision-making across various sectors. From market research to quality control, here are some key applications of business statistics:

1. **Market segmentation**

    Business statistics is utilized to cluster customers into distinct market segments according to their purchasing patterns, behavior, and demographics. For example, algorithms such as K-means clustering can classify customers based on income.

2. **Demand forecast**

    The application of techniques such as regression and time series is central in predicting future outcomes and demand. A time series analysis involves analyzing a sequence of data points collected or recorded at regular time intervals, which could reveal various cycles and patterns. These patterns and cycles are crucial for planning in the business environment.

3. **Customer satisfaction survey**

    Data collection instruments, such as questionnaires, are crucial for obtaining feedback from customers. Questionnaires are standard, structured documents with a series of questions for customers on a specific subject. Customers may be asked to share their views and suggestions, which could help improve the business. Online survey tools such as SurveyMonkey, Zoho Survey, and Qualtrics are available for this purpose.

4. Financial risk management

In order to evaluate and quantify risk, financial risk management frequently uses statistical techniques like probability and probability distributions. For example, client data is used by loan and microfinance organizations to predict the probability of prompt repayment or default. Institutions can categorize clients into various risk groups by modeling these probabilities, which helps them make judgments about whether to approve loans, set interest rates, or refuse credit services.

5. Quality control

There are various quality control tools in statistics, such as fishbone diagrams, Pareto charts, control charts, scatter diagrams, and others. These tools have wide applications in manufacturing and production sectors, where they are used to check whether processes are under control or not.

6. Performance analysis

Performance analysis looks at employees' Key Performance Indicators (KPIs) using statistical techniques. It gives managers, staff, and decision-makers information on deviations from the norm in addition to assisting observers in evaluating individual and team performance. These results encourage the creation of plans to boost output, coordinate activities with company objectives, and assist staff in achieving their goals.

7. Inventory management

It is crucial for a business to keep the right inventory. Overstocking and understocking need to be avoided as they could lead to loss of time and resources. Techniques such as linear programming and combinatorial optimization are useful to determine the right inventory levels.

8. A/B testing

A/B testing is a statistical technique that compares the performance of two versions of the same content to see which is more appealing to a webpage's visitors. Marketing campaigns on web pages can benefit from A/B testing. This tool works alongside digital solutions to test various elements of the marketing campaign and identify performing elements and those that are not doing well.

9. Financial review

Analyzing financial transactions can help detect anomalies and suspicious activities and point out appropriate steps to take to prevent fraud.

1.3 Importance of Business Statistics

The importance of business statistics goes beyond dealing with numbers. It has a pivotal role in determining the course and success of contemporary businesses.

Here are several key aspects that highlight the significance of business statistics:

1. Informed decision-making

Management can make well-informed decisions using business statistics, as it offers a methodical and impartial approach. It provides key stakeholders with data-backed information to assist them in navigating complexity, considering options, and making decisions that support business objectives.

2. Risk mitigation

Risk is a part of any business endeavor. Enterprises can estimate and quantify risks using statistical knowledge and make appropriate decisions.

3. Financial planning and forecasting

When it comes to forecasting income, planning expenses, or assessing investment prospects, statistical models offer a dependable structure for making prudent financial choices.

4. Resource optimization

In corporate operations, efficiency is critical. Business statistics helps to optimize the use of resources, including labor, capital, and time. This optimization increases output, reduces waste, and raises operational efficiency as a whole.

5. Market research and customer insights

As seen previously in Section 1.2, knowledge of business statistics is also vital in conducting market research and surveys to understand customer behavior and preferences.

| Figure 1.1 | Importance of business statistics |

In today's data-driven business environment, the importance of the right usage of statistics continues to grow. By assisting business-related data to be converted into insights for practice, business statistics ultimately helps firms succeed in the long term.

So far, we have explored the background, applications, and importance of business statistics. In the upcoming sections, we will explore the most commonly used and essential statistical terms before concluding with instances of potential statistical misuse.

1.4 Essential Terms in Statistics

In this section, we will briefly introduce and define the most frequently used concepts in business statistics. Let's begin:

1. **Data**

   This term refers to facts or figures, usually in numerical or categorical form, gathered through measurement or recording for analysis and presentation. Data may also be considered a systematic record of a given metric, essentially the raw information. For instance, when a vendor systematically records the daily profits for a given week.

2. **Information**

   It is the interpretation of insights drawn from the analysis of data. Unlike raw data or unstructured data, information is organized and puts such data into context. For a vendor, making daily recordings of weekly profits is data. However, using this data to identify the days of the week that had minimum and maximum profit levels is information. The vendor may then use this information to determine what factors contributed to the least and maximum profits and scale the business.

3. **Population**

   It refers to all the concerned units or items from which data is collected for study and analysis. Alternatively, it may be known as a group with shared characteristics that the researcher wants to learn more about.

4. **Sample**

It is a subset of the population whose items or units have been selected for study. A sample is usually assumed to represent the population being studied accurately.

Figure 1.2 Distinction between population and sample

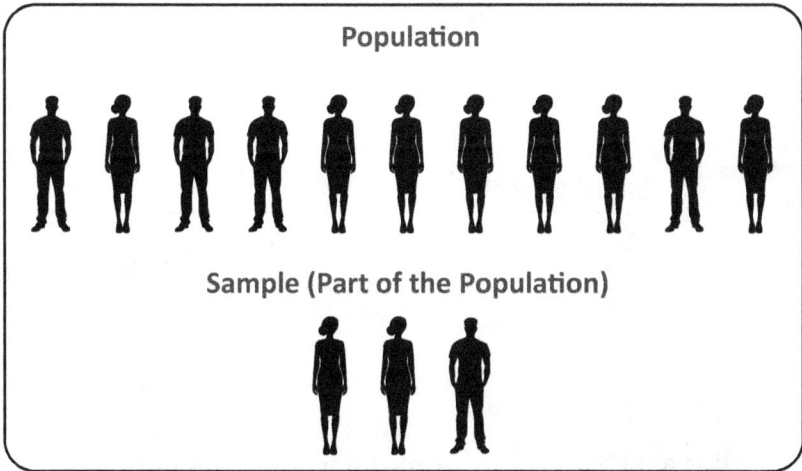

5. **Sample size**

It is the number of items or units, or individuals, included in a sample.

6. **Parameter vs. Statistics**

A parameter represents population characteristics, while statistics refer to numbers representing a sample's characteristics. An example of a parameter is the population mean, while the sample mean is a statistic. The symbol for the population mean is μ, while that for a sample mean is $\bar{x}$.

7. Descriptive statistics

Descriptive statistics involves calculating the summary statistics of a dataset with no specified degree of accuracy.

8. Inferential statistics

These are summary statistics calculated from samples drawn from populations. These statistics are generalized to the whole population, assuming that the sample is representative of the population.

Figure 1.3 Branches of statistics

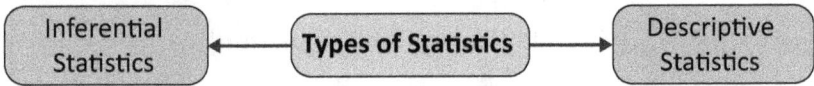

Inferential Statistics ← Types of Statistics → Descriptive Statistics

9. Hypothesis

It is a testable claim, proposition, or argument that is assumed to be true. It is tested using scientific research by collecting data, analyzing it, and drawing appropriate conclusions.

10. Probability

It is the likelihood that an outcome or event will occur in a given probability space, considering that the measure of the whole probability space is 1.

11. Outliers

These are extremely low or high values in a data set. In a dataset, outliers usually have an abnormal distance from the other values. In any dataset, though classification is often guided by statistical rules, final judgment may depend on the researcher's discretion.

12. Variable

A variable is a measurable or countable attribute, a characteristic, or quantity of an object or item. Data items such as gender, product size, product type, product number, and stock level are examples of variables.

Let us consider the example below to understand some of these key terms.

1.4.1 Example: Understanding essential terms in statistics

Let's say we are interested in finding out the average amount (mean) of money BizStat College second-year students spend on non-book educational materials. Suppose, out of a 100-student random sample, three students spent $160, $200, and $225. In this scenario, we can define some key terms discussed in the previous section as follows:

- The population is all second-year students attending BizStat College this term.

- The sample is 100 second-year students randomly selected for the survey. They are assumed to be representing the entire population of second-year students at BizStat College.

- The parameter is the average (mean) amount of money spent (excluding books) by second-year college students at BizStat College this term. This is the population mean.

- The statistic is the average (mean) amount of money spent (excluding books) by second-year college students in the sample.

- The variable could be the amount of money spent (excluding books) by one second-year student. Let X be the amount of money spent (excluding books) by one second-year student attending BizStat College.

- The data consists of the individual amounts spent by each of the 100 students in the sample. For example, three of these values are $160, $200, and $225.

1.5 Misuse of Statistics

While learning business statistics is vital for decision-making, it may be inappropriately used to mislead, persuade, influence, and deceive the masses. The misuse of statistics could be due to errors in research, poor analysis of data, selection of biased samples, poor labeling, forced comparison of unrelated items, and researcher bias, especially if they want to drive a particular ideology.

In business, data misuse could occur in scenarios where companies conduct surveys on their products and select a biased sample. Biased samples are likely to give false positive reviews of the products, influencing many people to buy the products. Deceitful companies gain profits by distorting the truth and propagating falsehoods in such a manner.

A famous case of misuse of statistics is the case of Colgate toothpaste brand advertising in the UK in 2007. The Advertising Standards Authority in the UK ordered Colgate to drop its slogan at the time, "More than 80% of dentists recommend Colgate," as it was seen to mislead consumers into believing that 80% of dentists in the UK recommended Colgate toothpaste while the remaining 20% did not (Clarke, 2007).

Following ethical research standards, selecting samples that are both random and representative, using acceptable statistical methods, and being transparent in data collecting and reporting are all crucial in preventing statistical misuse.

As we take on subsequent chapters, we will learn about the various concepts and practices that will help reduce the likelihood of misreporting or misusing statistics.

Concluding Chapter One, we take away an in-depth understanding of business statistics, its importance, and applications in various business segments. With this knowledge, we are well-prepared to be introduced to data in the next chapter, which is the backbone of business statistics.

Chapter Summary

- Business statistics is the art of gathering, evaluating, presenting, and organizing relevant data to support decision-making in the business environment.

- Raw data holds immense potential to transform the business environment when appropriate statistical techniques are employed.

- Business statistics has wide applications in various domains, including market segmentation, demand forecasting, customer satisfaction analysis, financial risk management, quality control, performance analysis, and inventory management.

- The knowledge of business statistics can help mitigate risk, financial planning, forecasting, resource optimization, performance evaluation, and making informed decisions in business.

- Essential terms in statistics include: data, variable, population, sample, and hypothesis. These terms will be frequently mentioned in the subsequent chapters of the book.

- Errors in research, biased samples, researcher bias, and poor analysis may be a source of misuse of statistics. To avoid statistical misuse, one must use random and representative samples, apply sound statistical methods, and keep a high level of transparency.

Further Learning

(Links also available in Online Resources)

1. **Application of statistics in daily life | Use and importance of statistics**
    http://bit.ly/45nM0XC

2. **How statistics can be misleading - Mark Liddell**
    http://bit.ly/3J8qiPN

Quiz

1. **Define business statistics:**
   a. The art of gathering, evaluating, presenting, and organizing relevant data to support decision-making in the business environment.
   b. It is the collection of data and comparing it with the data from competitors.
   c. It is a method used to forecast demands and sales in a business.

2. **How does business statistics aid in decision-making?**
   a. It has no impact on decision-making.
   b. It provides a systematic and objective approach to decision-making by offering a data-driven foundation.
   c. It only applies to financial decisions within a business.

3. **Provide examples of how business statistics is applied in different domains.**
   a. No practical applications in business
   b. Examples include market segmentation, demand forecasting, and customer satisfaction analysis
   c. Only applicable in financial risk management

4. **How does statistical analysis contribute to demand forecasting and market segmentation?**
   a. Statistical analysis has no role in these areas.
   b. It contributes by optimizing inventory and production planning, and by identifying and targeting specific customer segments.
   c. It contributes by predicting stock market trends.

5. **Enumerate the key aspects that highlight the significance of business statistics.**

   a. Business statistics is insignificant for decision-making.
   b. Its importance lies in misleading consumers.
   c. Business statistics can be applied in financial fraud detection.

6. **How does business statistics foster a culture of continuous improvement?**

   a. By discouraging organizations from analyzing their performance
   b. By analyzing available data and identifying areas for improvement and enhancement
   c. By providing tools for monitoring and reporting without any focus on improvement

7. **The following tools can be used by an e-commerce store to collect data on customer views and product feedback. Which one does not apply?**

   a. Zoho Survey
   b. Pareto chart
   c. SurveyMonkey

8. **Define the term "outlier" value.**

   a. An extremely low or high value in a dataset, lying at an abnormal distance from the other values
   b. A common value in a dataset
   c. A value that represents the average of a dataset

9. **What is a variable?**

   a. A variable is an object or item whose characteristics can be studied.
   b. A variable is a measurable or countable attribute, characteristic, or quantity of an object or item.
   c. A variable is a factor that changes in response to other factors.

10. **Differentiate between inferential and descriptive statistics.**

   a. Both terms refer to the same statistical approach.
   b. Descriptive statistics involves calculating summary statistics with no specified degree of accuracy, while inferential statistics involves using summaries to infer general characteristics of a population.
   c. Inferential statistics only applies to large datasets.

Answers

1 – a	2 – b	3 – b	4 – b	5 – c
6 – b	7 – b	8 – a	9 – b	10 – b

CHAPTER 2

Data Collection and Presentation

Key Learning Objectives

- Identify variables and their types.
- Explore the classification of data.
- Understand the scales used in the measurement of data.
- Learn the methods used in data collection.
- Dive into data presentation fundamentals.
- Explore ethical considerations in data collection.

We have discussed the importance of business statistics in Chapter One and seen how it heavily relies on data. In this chapter, you will be introduced to methods used to collect data and present it. The collection and presentation of data are fundamental to statistics, forming the backbone of strategic decision-making. Accurate data collection ensures the reliability of variables, classification, and measurement, while appropriate presentation methods, such as charts and graphs, make complex patterns accessible.

Understanding measurement scales, ethical considerations, and effective data collection methods allows businesses to draw meaningful insights, ensuring that statistical analysis is robust and ethically sound. By mastering these concepts, you will effectively analyze and communicate data to support strategic business objectives.

2.1 Variables and Types

A variable is a characteristic or attribute of an object or item that can be measured or observed and may take different forms. Data items such as gender, product size, product type, product number, and stock level are examples of variables.

The classification of variables is as follows:

1. **Dependent variable**

   It is the outcome or response in an experiment. This value is expected to change with dynamic independent variable levels. A good example is studying the impact of customer satisfaction on the monthly profit of a business. Monthly profit is a dependent variable whose changes are subject to variations in customer satisfaction.

2. **Independent variable**

   In an experiment, an independent variable is the variable that causes the effect or is responsible for the outcome in the dependent variable. This variable is also known as an explanatory or predictor variable. In the above example, with customer satisfaction and monthly profit, an independent variable is customer satisfaction. Changes in customer satisfaction explain the changes in the monthly profit of the business.

3. Extraneous variable

This is a variable that can impact results if it is not controlled. This variable is not usually part of the model or experiment, but significantly impacts the findings. The effects of extraneous variables need to be controlled in experiments to boost the chances of obtaining more accurate and reliable results.

In studying the effect of customer satisfaction on monthly profit, it can be found that factors such as product quality and other market conditions could impact the relationship. These factors are extraneous variables in the experiment and should be controlled to obtain accurate results.

2.2 Classification of Data

Classifying data involves organizing and categorizing data based on its qualities and characteristics. In statistics, the classification of data is essential as it enables one to make meaningful analyses and interpretations.

Figure 2.1 Classification of data in statistics

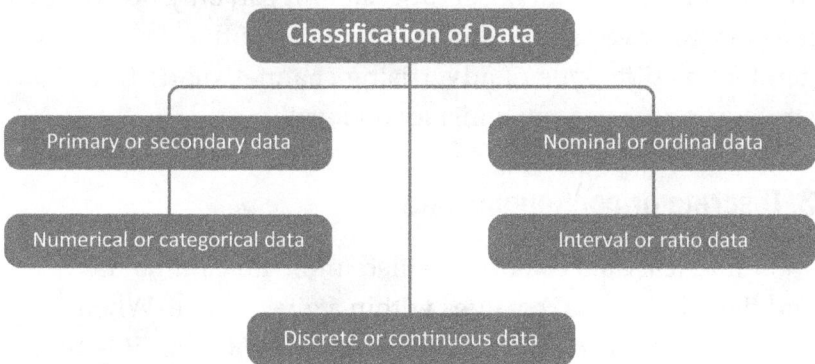

1. Primary or secondary data

This classification is based on the type of data source used to collect data. The main sources of primary data are those wherein researchers collect data firsthand, on their own, using surveys, observations, experiments, questionnaires, and interviews.

On the other hand, data from past records, collected by other researchers, which a researcher considers appropriate for their study, forms part of secondary data. The records containing secondary data may be extracted from public databases, government publications, or any other source containing data used in another study.

2. Numerical or categorical data

Numerical data refers to measurable or quantifiable attributes of an observational unit. They include numbers which allow mathematical operations, including addition, subtraction, division, and multiplication to be performed. Sales, profit, and the number of staff are examples of numerical data types.

Categorical or qualitative data refers to non-measurable attributes or characteristics of an observational unit. Such kind of data can only be descriptive. Categorical data means that an attribute of an observational unit can only be grouped into categories or a limited list. Examples of this data include gender, job title, type of advertising channel, marketing strategy, and customer satisfaction levels.

3. Discrete or continuous data

Numerical data can be classified into whole numbers and data that can take values within a given range. When numerical data can only take whole-number values, it is called discrete data. It is called continuous data when it takes values within a specified range. Discrete data values are positive integers, while continuous data have real numerical values.

4. Nominal or ordinal data

Categorical data can be classified further into nominal and ordinal data. When categorical data has a meaningful order, it is referred to as ordinal data. However, if the categories do not have an inherent order, it is referred to as nominal data.

The intervals for ordinal data are not uniform. Customer satisfaction levels (i.e., high, low, or medium) and customer ratings on products (1–5-star ratings) are examples of ordinal data. Gender, ethnicity, and job title of an employee in a business can be considered nominal data.

5. Interval or ratio data

Interval and Ratio data are measured along a scale with equal intervals. However, they differ slightly. Interval data does not have a true zero, while a ratio scale has a true zero. When a scale is said to have a true zero, it means that the value zero (0) represents absence.

Examples of interval data are time and temperature, while profits and sales are examples of ratio data. Temperature has an interval measure: 0, which does not mean that there is no temperature. However, for profit, a value of 0 in profits means that there is no attained profit.

2.3 Measurement Scales

After the classification of data, the next important aspect in data presentation is to determine how an observational unit's attributes are defined, measured, or grouped. Measurement scales are tools that support this process.

Depending on the data being handled, an appropriate measurement scale is chosen.

Let us look at the various types of measurement scales used in statistics:

1. Nominal scale

A variable is measured on a nominal scale by assigning labels or numbers to uniquely identify it. This scale does not assign a rank to the labels or numbers. A variable can be measured on the nominal scale if it has two or more levels, with no evaluative distinction.

An example of a variable that can be measured on this scale is gender. When coding the gender variable in data collection, the numbers 0 and 1 are commonly used to represent female and male participants. In this example, neither male nor female is greater than the other. Male and female are categories or levels of the gender variable.

2. Ordinal scale

An ordinal scale measures a variable by categorizing it into levels or ranks that can be ordered. However, these levels or ranks do not have uniform intervals between them. It is crucial to remember that the numbers allocated to a variable for its levels or categories do not correspond to the levels' numerical value or magnitude.

An example of a variable that can be measured on this scale is customer ratings for a product. A 5-star rating is better than or higher than a 1-star rating. A product that receives a majority of 5 stars performs well, unlike a 1-star rated product.

3. Interval scale

An interval scale provides a lot more information than an ordinal scale. This scale assigns numerical values at equal intervals to items or objects being measured. This scale, however, lacks a true zero, making it impossible to measure the absence of an attribute. Variables like temperature, potential of hydrogen (pH), Scholastic Assessment Test (SAT) scores, Intelligence Quotient (IQ), and credit scores can all be measured with the interval scale.

Microfinance businesses rely on their customers' credit scores in issuing loans and other credit services. However, when comparing customers' credit scores, the fact that one customer's credit score is half that of another does not mean that the latter is twice as creditworthy. Similarly, having no credit score does not imply that a customer is unreliable.

4. Ratio scale

A ratio scale has a true zero and assigns values to items or objects as numbers on a uniform scale. When the value of an attribute is zero, it means that the attribute is missing or absent. Variables such as weight, height, and distance can be measured on this scale.

2.4 Methods Used for Data Collection

The process of gathering data for a study or research entails the utilization of various techniques and methods. Depending on the kind of study being done, the data's structure, and the researcher's resources—including time and money—each method the researcher chooses is distinct.

1. Observations

Observations require the enumerator to visually capture data by observing and recording a phenomenon's events, attributes, and characteristics in its natural setting. Variables such as the type of vehicle, house design, and product color can be collected using the observation method.

2. Focus groups

A focus group is a data collection method that combines observations, surveys, and interviews of individuals with common characteristics. Focus groups widely use open-ended questions.

3. Records

It involves collecting data from recorded documents such as minutes from past meetings, registers, and other historical records.

4. Measurement

Researchers may use measuring equipment on participants or study items to measure the variables of interest in the study. Data on variables such as height, weight, temperature, and atmospheric pressure cannot be collected using other methods discussed previously except by measurement.

5. Triangulation method

It is a method of data collection that combines various data sources in a study. Using multiple sources to collect data enables the researcher to validate the accuracy of the data.

Different samples and data collections may be used to study the same phenomenon or answer the same research objectives. The time for the collection of data may also be varied.

A good example is interviewing a husband and wife separately on matters related to their family. This is triangulation involving different sources where the researcher seeks to compare responses and ascertain the validity of the responses.

Advantages of triangulation

A. Using multiple sources and methods to collect data limits the researcher's bias.

B. The validity of the findings is high.

C. Triangulating the subject under study enhances deeper understanding.

D. The use of many methods may bring about different angles of approaching the same problem.

E. The researcher is ultimately more confident with the collected data.

Disadvantages of triangulation

A. A lot of time is used to collect data.

B. A lot of resources are used in combining different sources.

C. Combining qualitative and quantitative methods can increase complexity and may affect consistency if not well integrated.

D. The researcher must have large samples to realize a higher statistical power.

E. Triangulation increases the complexity of the study.

6. Questionnaires

A questionnaire is a type of research instrument with a series of questions for respondents. The questions may begin with collecting personal information, followed by questions surrounding the views and opinions about a certain subject or topic that the investigator is interested in. A questionnaire may have verbal or written questions and closed or open-ended questions. It may be answered by the respondent or with the help of an enumerator in circumstances where respondents are illiterate or unable to write and read.

The use of questionnaires is the most common in surveys as they are less expensive and easier to use.

The enumerator may physically send the questionnaires to participants via courier services, and the participants return them after responding. Alternatively, the questionnaires may be sent using electronic services such as Gmail.

Successful questionnaires are usually accompanied by letters of introduction that outline the research process, the research's benefits, and the benefits that the respondents may get from the study. The investigator needs to guarantee the confidentiality and privacy of the respondents' responses. Questions in the questionnaire should be easy to understand.

Qualities of a good questionnaire

A. Questions that are sensitive to the participants should be avoided. The inclusion of sensitive questions may make participants uneasy and conceal important information.

B. Each question in the questionnaire should be aimed at answering or addressing a research objective.

C. Restricted or closed-ended questions should be preferred over open-ended ones to avoid complexity in analysis.

D. A question should not contain the use of double negatives.

E. Ambiguous questions should be avoided.

F. Only ask questions that are relevant to the study.

G. Biased questions or leading questions should be avoided.

Advantages of using questionnaires

A. There is uniformity in the responses as respondents answer the same questions.

B. There is less risk of bias as respondents answer the questions themselves.

C. It is inexpensive.

D. Regardless of the distance to the respondents, questionnaires can be sent electronically or by courier services.

Disadvantages of using questionnaires

A. Questionnaires may have high non-response rates.

B. Open-ended questions may bring about inaccurate data.

7. Interviews

This method involves the enumerator asking questions face-to-face or by telephone while recording the responses. This method collects primary data or follow-ups on participants during a study. In business, this method can be used to collect data on customer satisfaction or feedback on certain products. A translator may be used when the interviewer and the interviewees have differences in language.

Advantages of interviews

A. Accurate information is collected.

   B. It is suitable when collecting data from a small geographical area with few participants.

   C. A researcher has the power to control the sample in the best interest of the study.

   D. Researchers can create rapport with respondents, motivating them to provide accurate information.

   E. Interviews can be used to collect sensitive data from respondents.

Disadvantages of interviews

   A. The researcher's ability to control samples may open a window to influence the results, leading to the researcher's bias.

   B. A lot of time and resources are used to meet every single interviewee.

   C. Interviews are limited to small geographical areas. It is challenging to apply them to large geographical areas.

   D. A researcher may quickly develop stereotypes, thereby leading to bias.

2.5 Ethical Considerations in Data Collection

Every time researchers go out in the field to conduct research, they are usually guided by a set of standards and regulations known as research ethics. They are as follows:

   1. Research participants should give their consent before giving out data.

   2. Participants should be respected.

   3. There should be transparency.

   4. The researcher should assure the participants of confidentiality and privacy.

5. The researcher should ensure that there are no potential risks of harm.

6. Participants' data should be stored securely.

7. The researcher should strive to attain reliability and validity.

2.6 Data Presentation

After the collection of data, it is crucial to organize it in a readable and understandable format. Data presentation implies using charts and graphs to display collected data. Presenting data using these tools enables effective communication of findings to stakeholders who may not have statistical knowledge.

Various methods, such as bar charts, pie charts, histograms, frequency polygons, and ogives, are used for this purpose. Each chosen chart or graph is unique, and its selection also depends on the data to be displayed. Let's look at them one by one:

1. Histogram

A histogram involves representing the frequencies of quantitative data using rectangular bars. The height of each bar represents the frequency of data in each category. These categories are usually plotted on the horizontal axis, while the frequencies of each category are plotted on the vertical axis.

A histogram can reveal the distribution of data, whether normal or skewed. Normally distributed data will have the histogram's peak at the center. Skewed distributions have their tails either to the right or left.

A histogram can be made in tools such as Microsoft Excel using the Data Analysis option. In a business setup, it is utilized to display frequencies of website load times, performance assessment, employee age distribution, and time taken to attend to customers.

When to use a histogram:

- When you are dealing with continuous data that needs to be grouped into ranges or bins (e.g., stock levels, employee ages, customer wait times).
- When you want to understand the distribution of data, whether it's skewed, normal, or uniform.
- When you are interested in the frequency of data points within specific intervals or ranges.

Let us consider the following hypothetical data from Mark's Company. The data contains the average time in minutes taken to attend to a customer and the frequency of employees within each time interval.

Table 2.1   Average attendance time and frequency of employees

Average time taken to attend to a customer (in minutes)	Number of employees (frequency)
0–9	3
10–19	10
20–29	6
30–39	4
40–49	2
50–59	0

Figure 2.2	Histogram of average attendance time in Mark's company

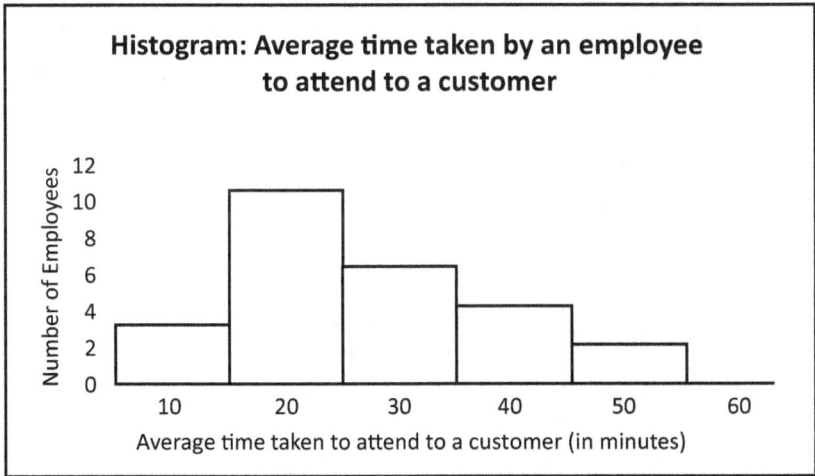

Histogram: Average time taken by an employee to attend to a customer

2. Frequency polygon

A frequency polygon is a line graph of class frequencies plotted on the vertical axis against the midpoints of classes on the horizontal axis. In Excel, a frequency polygon can be created by holding the ALT button and pressing N-N-1 on the keyboard. Right-click on the chart to "Select Data." Drag the frequencies column towards the series values and the midpoint of the classes towards the category axis.

This graph can be applied in business settings to compare sales trends over time, track website traffic, assess performance, and delivery times.

When to use a frequency polygon:

- You need to compare multiple data sets simultaneously.
- You want a clearer visualization of trends or distributions over a continuous range.

- You prefer a less cluttered alternative to overlapping histograms.

Using data on "customer attendance time" of employees from Mark's company, we can make a frequency polygon shown below:

Figure 2.3 Frequency polygon of average attendance time in Mark's company

Frequency polygon: Average time taken by an employee to attend to a customer

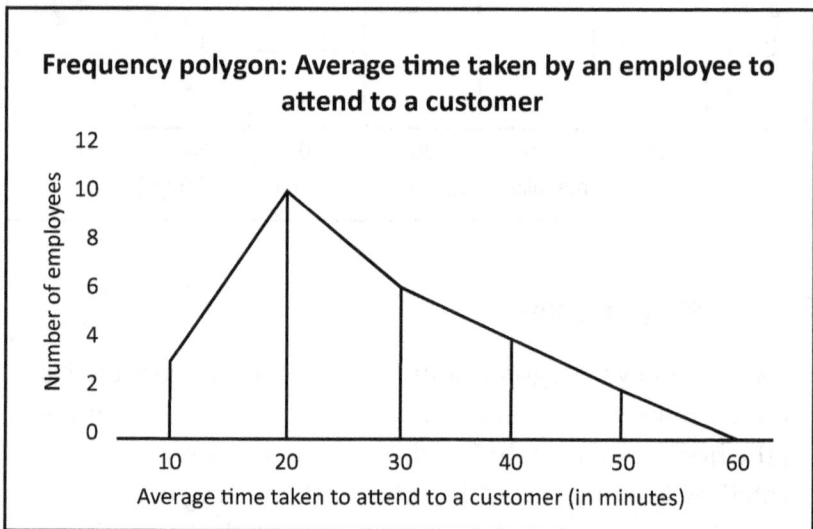

3. Ogive

An ogive is a line graph of the cumulative frequencies against the upper-class boundaries of the classes. In Excel, an ogive can be created by holding the ALT button and pressing N-N-1 on the keyboard. Right-click on the chart to "Select Data." Drag the cumulative frequencies column towards the series values and the upper boundaries of the classes towards the category axis.

Ogives can be applied to display cumulative defect rates of a product, cumulative sales and profits, cumulative wait times for customers in a queue, and cumulative inventory turnover days (e.g., 0–15 days, 16–31 days).

When to use an ogive:

- When you want to display cumulative data to show how totals build up over intervals.
- When you need to identify thresholds, such as the point at which 50% or 80% of the data is accumulated.
- When the data involves ranges or intervals, and cumulative frequency is of interest.

Using data on "customer attendance time" of employees from Mark's company, we can make an ogive as shown in Figure 2.4 below. The cumulative frequency is anchored at 0 so that the curve begins at 0.

Figure 2.4 **An ogive of average attendance time in Mark's company**

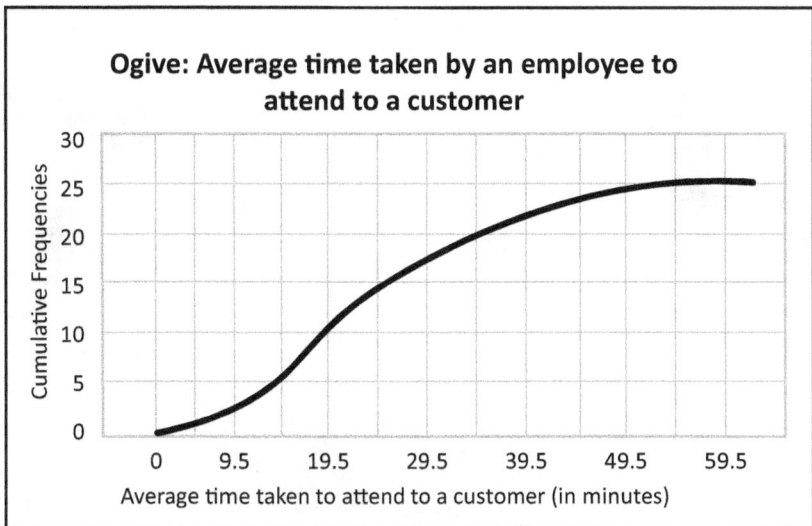

Ogive: Average time taken by an employee to attend to a customer

4. Pie chart

Pie charts are circular graphical data presentation tools divided into sections, with each section representing a numerical proportion. The keyboard shortcut ALT-N-Q is used to create a pie chart in Excel. Right-click on the chart to "Select Data." Drag the frequencies column towards the series values and the classes towards the category axis.

We can use the same example of customer attendance data to create a pie chart in Excel. Pie charts can be utilized to display the proportion of market share of a business, the distribution of expenses, and the sales and profits of stores in a chain.

When to use a pie chart:

- The data represents parts of a whole (e.g., percentages or proportions).
- You want to show relative sizes or contributions.
- The categories are limited in number (usually no more than 5–7).

Figure 2.5 Pie chart of average attendance time in Mark's company

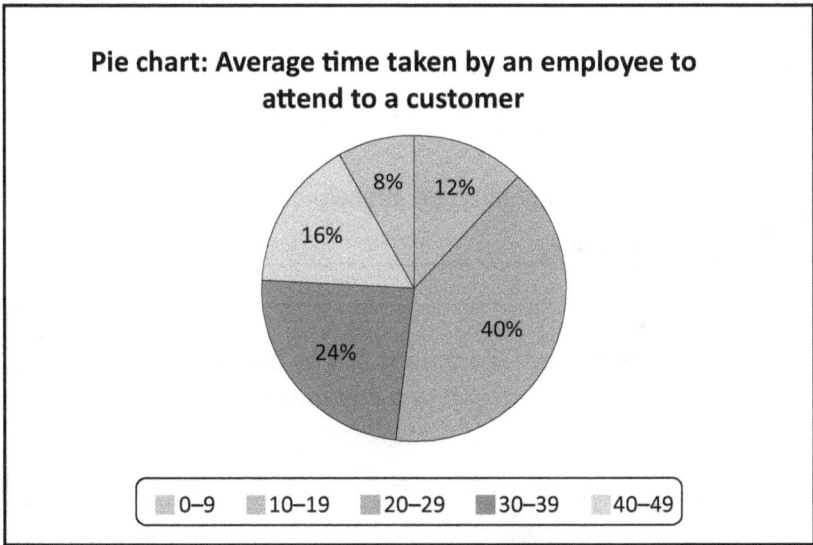

Pie chart: Average time taken by an employee to attend to a customer

8% 12%

16%

40%

24%

0–9   10–19   20–29   30–39   40–49

5. Bar chart

Bar charts are used to display categorical data in the form of rectangular bars. Each bar on the horizontal axis represents a class or group, while the height of each bar represents the count or frequency of the class plotted on the vertical axis.

Bar charts can be created in Excel by navigating to the "Insert>>Bar chart" and choosing a clustered column chart under the charts section. Some applications of bar charts include: displaying market share, sales by stores or regions, and product profit by category.

When to use a bar chart:

- When you are comparing discrete categories (e.g., different regions, products, or time periods).

- When you need to show differences between categories in a clear and easily interpretable way.
- When the number of categories is manageable (usually 5–10 categories).
- When you want to display trends over time (e.g., using a vertical bar chart for time series data).

Figure 2.6 Bar chart of average attendance time in Mark's company

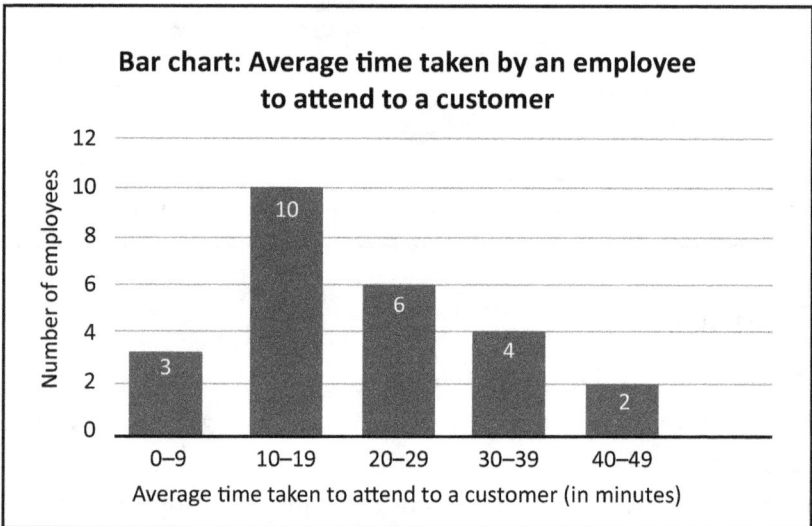

Bar chart: Average time taken by an employee to attend to a customer

Through this chapter, you have learned the concepts of data collection and presentation, from understanding what a variable is and its classification to exploring the various measurement scales and methods of data collection. This means that you are now equipped to gather, organize, and present data effectively. You will also be able to adhere to ethical practices as you collect and organize your data.

The next chapter will introduce how to begin data analysis by understanding descriptive statistics and learning how to calculate its measures.

Chapter Summary

- Data is categorized as primary/secondary, numerical/ categorical, discrete/continuous, nominal/ordinal, or interval/ratio data.

- Nominal, ordinal, interval, and ratio measurement scales are used based on properties like ranking and the presence of a true zero. Each scale serves different purposes in data representation.

- Understanding measurement scales is crucial for choosing appropriate statistical analyses.

- Questionnaires, interviews, observations, focus groups, records, measurements, and triangulation are methods used to collect data.

- Triangulation enhances data validity and provides a comprehensive understanding, but it requires careful planning.

- Data can be visually presented using histograms, frequency polygons, ogives, pie charts, and bar charts.

- Choosing the right graph depends on the nature of the data.

- Researchers must obtain participant consent, respect their rights, ensure transparency, and guarantee confidentiality.

- Ethical principles guide fair and responsible research conduct.

Further Learning

(Links also available in Online Resources)

1. **Data collection: Understanding the types of data**
   http://bit.ly/40XiGpE
2. **Measurement scales**
   http://bit.ly/4mdcmCV
3. **Data presentation**
   http://bit.ly/4oB7r0i

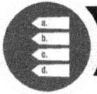

Quiz

1. In a retail business, which of the following is an example of qualitative data?

    a. Sales revenue
    b. Number of sold products
    c. Customer satisfaction rating

2. A restaurant manager wants all served customers to rate their services before leaving. He develops a short customer survey and customers are required to rate the services on a scale of 1 to 5 (5 = highest satisfaction level and 1 = least satisfaction level). Identify the type of measurement scale the manager used.

    a. Nominal
    b. Ordinal
    c. Interval

3. For an online bookstore, which of the following is a quantitative variable?

    a. Book genre
    b. Customer feedback
    c. Book price

4. What is a key ethical consideration when collecting customer data for a business?

    a. Minimizing data accuracy
    b. Ensuring data privacy and security
    c. Collecting data without consent

5. A company wants to ensure the reliability of its employee satisfaction survey. What is a recommended practice?

   a. Limit the sample size to a few employees.

   b. Use biased survey questions.

   c. Provide anonymity to respondents.

6. A smartphone manufacturing company wants to know what customers say about their latest smartphone release. Specifically, they are more concerned with views on the attributes below. Which of them is a qualitative attribute?

   a. The size of the smartphone

   b. Price of the smartphone

   c. The quality of the sound from the speakers

7. What is an independent variable in a study or experiment?

   a. A variable with uniform intervals

   b. A variable influencing the dependent variable

   c. A variable measured on a nominal scale

8. Which of the following is an example of categorical data?

   a. Sales revenue

   b. Temperature

   c. Customer satisfaction level (Low, Average, High)

9. What type of scale lacks a true zero but has equal intervals between measurements?

   a. Nominal

   b. Interval

   c. Ratio

10. In data collection, what is primary data based on?

    a. Existing records

    b. Previous studies

    c. Firsthand research

Answers

1 – c	2 – b	3 – c	4 – b	5 – c
6 – c	7 – b	8 – c	9 – b	10 – c

CHAPTER 3

Descriptive Statistics

>
>
> ### Key Learning Objectives
>
> - Calculate and interpret measures of central tendency.
> - Examine measures of the middle.
> - Understand the general properties of measures of the middle and measures of central tendency.
> - Analyze and apply measures of dispersion.

At this point, you have an idea of the importance of business statistics and have been familiarized with data collection and presentation. After you have collected your data and presented it using the methods described in the previous chapter, you may want to summarize it. These summaries provide insights before you analyze and test your hypotheses, as we will see in upcoming chapters.

In this chapter, you will be introduced to the concept of "descriptive statistics." Descriptive statistics serve as the basis for all statistical analyses. They help to determine the summary characteristics of a variable. Keep in mind that data can be either non-numerical (such product categories, employee satisfaction levels, or client preferences) or numerical (like sales numbers, expenses, or production volumes).

By understanding how to arrive at central tendency (mean, median, mode) and dispersion (range, variance, standard deviation) measures, you will have the knowledge to summarize and gain insights on any given data.

3.1 Measures of Central Tendency

The measures of central tendency help to determine the center of a distribution. The mean, median, and mode are the most common measures of the center.

3.1.1 Mean

The mean is the average of all the data values in a dataset. It is obtained by summing all the values and dividing this sum by the number of values.

Recall the understanding of sample and population as discussed in Chapter One, Section 1.4. In statistics, the mean for a sample is represented by the symbol, while μ is used to signify the population mean.

Let's suppose you have a dataset, X, and its data values can be written as X1 to Xn, i.e., X1, X2, X3,..., Xn, where Xn is the last data value and X1 is the first data value in the dataset or record. The mean of the dataset can be found through the addition of all the X1, X2, X3,..., Xn values, and then dividing by the number of values in the dataset X represented by n. The summation of all data values is represented by the Greek symbol $\sum$.

Therefore, the sum of all values of X is $\sum X$ given as:

$$\sum_{i=1}^{n} X_i = X1 + X2 + X3 + X4 + ..., + Xn,$$ where n is the total number of data values and X_i denotes each individual data value.

Sample mean: $\bar{x} = \dfrac{\sum_{i=1}^{n} x_i}{n}$

Population mean: $\mu = \dfrac{\sum_{i=1}^{N} X_i}{N}$

"N" is the number of values or items in a population, while "n" is the number of items in a sample.

Means can be applied in business environments, for instance, to obtain the average cost of production of items in a factory, the average business spending in a month, the average number of customers attended to in a day, and/or average sales revenue in a month.

Example

Suppose the dataset X has the values 10, 20, 18, 14, 19, 19, 18, 20, 17, 18 such that X = {10, 20, 18, 14, 19, 19, 18, 20, 17, 18}. Determine the mean for the dataset X.

Solution

$$\bar{x} = \frac{\sum_{i=1}^{n} x_i}{n}$$

$$\sum_{i=1}^{10} x_i = 10 + 20 + 18 + 14 + 19 + 19 + 18 + 20 + 17 + 18 = 173$$

$$\bar{x} = \frac{173}{10} = 17.3$$

In Excel, the mean can be obtained by putting the number of days in a range, say A1:A10, and using the formula below:

= AVERAGE (A1:A10)

3.1.2 Median

A median value is the middle value when data is arranged in ascending or descending order. A median divides the values of a dataset into equal halves such that 50% of the dataset falls below or above it. If the dataset has an odd number of values, it is easy to pick the median as the middle value. However, the median of a dataset with an even number of values is the average of the two numbers in the middle. The symbol for the median is "M."

Enterprises can rely on the median, where the mean is affected by extreme values. An example is when analyzing customer satisfaction ratings, the median score offers a robust central value that isn't influenced by extreme positive or negative ratings.

Example A

Consider the dataset below for the number of phones manufactured by 7 companies in January. Determine the median number of phones manufactured by the 7 companies in January.

1900, 1242, 1678, 1867, 1546, 1763, 1000

Solution

Let's start by sorting the numbers in ascending order:
Ascending order: 1000, 1242, 1546, 1678, 1763, 1867, 1900

The middle value in the arranged data values is 1678. Therefore, the median (M) = 1678

The median can also be obtained in Excel using the command below (assuming that the data values are in the range F1:F7).

= MEDIAN (F1:F7)

The above formula returns the value of 1678, which is the median for the number of phones manufactured by the 7 companies in January.

Example B

The records at the finance department in a company show that the Chief Executive Officer (CEO) earns $5,500,000 while other staff earn $35,000 each. There are 50 people in the company, including the CEO. Between the mean and median salaries, which is a better measure of the "center?"

Solution

Mean salary $\bar{x} = \dfrac{\sum\limits_{i=1}^{n} x_i}{n}$

Total earnings, $\sum\limits_{i=1}^{n} x_i = 5{,}500{,}000 + 49(35{,}000) = \$7{,}215{,}000$

Let us now divide the total earnings by the total number of people, n.

$\bar{x} = \dfrac{7{,}215{,}000}{50} = \$144{,}300$

The median, M = $35,000, since arranging the earnings in either descending or ascending order gives $35,000 as the middle value.

The median is a better measure than the mean since most of the employees, 49, earn $35,000 while only one individual, the CEO, earns $5,500,000.

3.1.3 Mode

A mode is the most repeated or occurring data value in a dataset. Datasets may have more than one mode value. A unimodal dataset has one mode, a bimodal dataset has two, and a multimodal dataset has more than two modes. If a dataset does not have a mode value, it is incorrect to say that its mode is 0 because zero is a number.

To calculate the mode in Excel, the command below is used: MODE.MULT(A1:A7)

This command returns the most occurring data value (mode), and where the dataset does not have a mode, the value #N/A is returned.

The mode can be used by businesses to determine a product's popularity, most common customer preferences, and popular pricing levels.

Example A

Calculate the mean, mode, and median for the sample of stock prices drawn from the two companies below.

Table 3.1	Stock prices drawn from two companies								
StatEdge Electronics	27	25	26	30	35	25	29	30	30	28
BizStat Insights	42	38	40	42	41	38	39	40	43	41

Solution

StatEdge Electronics:

Mean stock price for StatEdge Electronics:

$$\bar{x} = \frac{\sum_{i=1}^{n} x_i}{n}$$

$$\bar{x} = \frac{(27 + 25 + 26 + 30 + 35 + 25 + 29 + 30 + 30 + 28)}{10}$$

$$\bar{x} = \frac{285}{10} = \$28.5$$

StatEdge Electronics' stock prices in ascending order are: (25, 25, 26, 27, 28, 29, 30, 30, 30, 35)

The middle values are 28 and 29.

Therefore, the median stock price value is $\frac{28 + 29}{2} = \$28.5$

The mode for StatEdge Electronics is $30.

BizStat Insights:

Mean Stock Price for BizStat Insights:

$$\bar{x} = \frac{\sum\limits_{i=1}^{n} x_i}{n}$$

$$\bar{x} = \frac{(38 + 39 + 40 + 40 + 40 + 41 + 41 + 42 + 42 + 43)}{10}$$

$$\bar{x} = \frac{406}{10} = \$40.6$$

The BizStat Insights Stock prices in ascending order are: (38, 39, 40, 40, 40, 41, 41, 42, 42, 43).

The middle values are 40 and 41. Therefore, the median stock price value is: $\frac{40 + 41}{2} = 40.5$.

The mode for BizStat Insights is $40.

| Figure 3.1 | Output of descriptive statistics in Excel |

StatEdge Analytics	(x-R)	(x-R)^2		BizStat Insights	(x-R)	(x-R)^2
27	-1.5	2.25		42	1.4	1.96
25	-3.5	12.25		38	-2.6	6.76
26	-2.5	6.25		40	-0.6	0.36
30	1.5	2.25		42	1.4	1.96
35	6.5	42.25		41	0.4	0.16
25	-3.5	12.25		40	-0.6	0.36
29	0.5	0.25		39	-1.6	2.56
30	1.5	2.25		40	-0.6	0.36
30	1.5	2.25		43	2.4	5.76
28	-0.5	0.25		41	0.4	0.16
Sum	0	82.5		Sum	0	20.4

Descriptive Statistics

Input
Input Range: $G$5:$G$15
Grouped By: ● Columns ○ Rows
☑ Labels in first row

Output options
● Output Range: $G$21
○ New Worksheet Ply:
○ New Workbook
☑ Summary statistics
☐ Confidence Level for Mean: 95 %
☐ Kth Largest: 1
☐ Kth Smallest: 1

OK | Cancel | Help

StatEdge Analytics	
Mean	28.5
Standard Error	0.957427108
Median	28.5
Mode	30
Standard Deviation	3.027650354

BizStat Insights	
Mean	40.6
Standard Error	0.476095229
Median	40.5
Mode	40
Standard Deviation	1.505545305

The output returns the measures of central tendency discussed above and measures of dispersion such as the standard deviation and the variance. We will explore the mentioned measures of dispersion in-depth as part of Section 3.4.

Example B

21 students in a business statistics class scored the following marks in their end of year exam: 50, 53, 59, 59, 59, 63, 63, 72, 72, 72, 72, 72, 76, 78, 81, 83, 84, 84, 84, 90, and 93. Find the mode.

Solution

The most occurring score is 72. It occurs five times. Therefore, the mode among the 21 business statistics scores is 72.

In Excel, the three measures of central tendency can be obtained using the "DATA ANALYSIS" feature. To do this in Excel, go to Data>> Data Analysis>> Descriptive Statistics. Input the correct range for the data values for each dataset and choose an appropriate output range. Repeat for the other dataset.

3.2 Measures of the Middle

Apart from the measures of central tendency, there are other measures of the middle. These measures include:

1. Mid-range
2. Weighted mean
3. Measures of grouped data

3.2.1 Mid-range

A mid-range represents the average value between the maximum and the minimum values in a dataset.

$$\text{Mid-range} = \frac{minimum\{dataset\} + maximum\{dataset\}}{2}$$

The mid-range can give a quick estimate of the balance point between the highest and lowest stock quantities, aiding in inventory planning.

Example

Consider the number of customers who visit a mall, recorded for all 7 days of the first week of January. Calculate the mid-range number of customers for the week.

Solution

{236, 278, 455, 786, 250, 224, 564}

$$\text{Mid-range} = \frac{224 + 786}{2} = 505$$

The mid-range value can be obtained in Excel, assuming the data values are in the range A1:A8, using the formula:

= [MIN(A1:A8) + MAX(A1:A8)] / 2

3.2.2 Weighted mean

This type of mean involves multiplying each data value in a dataset by its corresponding weight and dividing the sum of the products by the sum of the weights.

$$\overline{x} = \frac{\sum_{i=1}^{n} w_i x_i}{\sum_{i=1}^{n} w_i}$$, where x_i represents the ith data value and w_i

the weight of the ith data value.

The sum of all weights adds up to 1 if the weights are given as decimals. If they are given as a percentage (e.g., 44%), then the sum of all the weights should be 100%.

When the weights are equal for the data values, the weighted mean usually collapses to the usual arithmetic mean.

A weighted mean can be used for a business that has many chain stores to analyze sales revenue across multiple stores. The calculated weighted mean accounts for the varying contribution of each store based on its sales volume. Additionally, it can also be utilized to calculate key performance indicators (KPIs) that measure success in an organization and evaluate customer feedback.

Example A

A student takes three 100-mark business statistics exams in a semester. The student scored 87, 86, and 99 in the three exams. The professor observes that the last exam was easier compared to the first two and therefore assigns it less weight. The weights assigned for each exam are given in Table 3.2 below:

| Table 3.2 | The weights assigned for each exam |

Business statistics exams	Student score (x)	Weight (w)
Exam 1	87	44%
Exam 2	86	44%
Exam 3	99	12%

What is the weighted average score for the student?

Solution

The formula for the weighted average: $\bar{x} = \dfrac{\sum\limits_{i=1}^{n} w_i x_i}{\sum\limits_{i=1}^{n} w_i}$

We know that the sum of the weights must be 1. Let's make sure that it is true for the problem above:

$44\% \Rightarrow 0.44,\ 12\% \Rightarrow 0.12$

$(0.44*2) + 0.12 = 1$

Therefore, we can calculate the sum of the product of marks (x_i) and the associated weights (w_i) as:

$\sum\limits_{i=1}^{n} w_i x_i = (87*44) + (86*44) + (99*12) = 8800$

$\sum\limits_{i=1}^{n} w_i = 44\% + 44\% + 12\% = 100\%$

$\bar{x} = \dfrac{8800}{100} = 88$

Thus, the weighted mean mark for the student is 88.

The SUMPRODUCT function is used in Excel to calculate the weighted mean. Suppose that the marks above are in the range B2:B4 and the weights are in the range C2:C4. The weighted mean can be calculated by the formula below:

= SUMPRODUCT(B2:B4, C2:C4) / SUM(C2:C4)

Figure 3. **Calculating weighted mean in Excel**

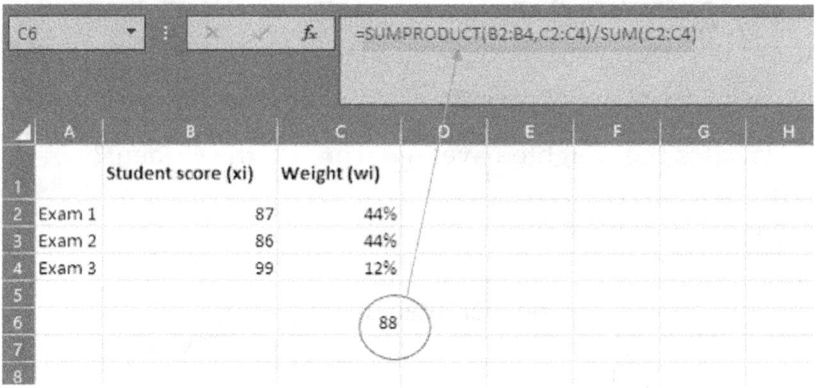

Example B

At the beginning of the year, Duncan buys 100 shares in an insurance company at $10 per share. In July, he decided to buy an additional 50 shares at $40. What is the weighted average price paid by Duncan to purchase the shares in that year?

Solution

The weighted average is $\bar{x} = \dfrac{\sum\limits_{i=1}^{n} w_i x_i}{\sum\limits_{i=1}^{n} w_i}$, x_i represents the price of shares and w_i represents the number of shares.

$$\bar{x} = \$\left(\frac{(100 * 10) + (50 * 40)}{100 + 50}\right) = \$\left(\frac{3000}{150}\right) = \$20$$

The total number of shares that Duncan has is 150 shares, and the weighted average price for each is $20.

Example C

A factory purchases 20,000 units of electricity at $1 each, 15,000 at $1.15 each, and 5,000 at $2 each over 8 months. Calculate the weighted price of the electricity units purchased by the factory.

Solution

The formula for the weighted average is: $\bar{x} = \dfrac{\sum\limits_{i=1}^{n} w_i x_i}{\sum\limits_{i=1}^{n} w_i}$,

x_i representing the price of each unit, and w_i is the number of electricity units purchased.

$$\bar{x} = \frac{\sum\limits_{i=1}^{n} w_i x_i}{\sum\limits_{i=1}^{n} w_i} = \$\left(\frac{(20{,}000^{*}1) + (15{,}000^{*}1.15) + (5{,}000^{*}2)}{20{,}000 + 15{,}000 + 5{,}000} \right)$$

$\bar{x} = \$1.18$

3.2.3 Measures of grouped data

Grouped data are organized into classes, and the frequencies for each class are provided. The classes are usually organized from the lowest class to the highest class. Provided with such data, we can calculate the mean and determine the modal class.

To calculate the mean for grouped data, the following formula is applied:

$$\bar{x} = \frac{\sum_{i=1}^{n} f_i (x_m)_i}{n}$$, where $f_i \Rightarrow$ class frequency, $(x_m) \Rightarrow$ midpoint

of the class, and n is the sum of all the frequencies.

Example

In Mark's company, there are 25 employees. Each employee takes a different amount of time to attend to a customer in their department. The distribution of the time taken to attend to customers by employees is shown in the table below.

Table 3.3   **The distribution of employee response time to customers**

Time taken to attend to a customer (in minutes)	Number of employees (frequency)
0–9	3
10–19	10
20–29	6
30–39	4
40–49	2
50–59	0

Solution

Step 1: Finding the midpoint for each class

For 0–9, the midpoint is 4.5.

For 10–19, the midpoint is 14.5.

For 20–29, the midpoint is 24.5.

For 30–39, the midpoint is 34.5.

For 40–49, the midpoint is 44.5.

For 50–59, the midpoint is 54.5.

Step 2: Multiply each midpoint by the frequency for the class

For 0–9, (4.5)(3) = 13.5

For 10–19, (14.5)(10) = 145

For 20–29, (24.5)(6) = 147

For 30–39, (34.5)(4) = 138

For 40–49,(44.5)(2) = 89

For 50–59, (54.5)(0) = 0

The addition of the product of frequencies and the midpoint (13.5 + 145 + 147 + 138 + 89) gives 532.5.

Therefore,

$$\bar{x} = \frac{\sum_{i=1}^{n} f_i(x_m)_i}{n} = \frac{532.5}{25} = 21.3 \text{ minutes}$$

The mean time an employee attends to a customer is 21.3 minutes.

The modal class from the distribution is the class with the highest frequency. In the distribution used above, the modal class is 10–19. To get the mode, the midpoint of the modal class is taken, which is 14.5.

The median class can be determined by calculating cumulative frequencies as shown in Table 3.4 below.

Table 3.4	Cumulative frequencies	

Attendance times (Classes)	Number of employees (frequency)	Cumulative frequency
0–9	3	3
10–19	10	13
20–29	6	19
30–39	4	23
40–49	2	25
50–59	0	25

The total number of employees in Mark's Company is 25 (n = 25), and half the number of these employees is 13. From the cumulative frequency column in the table above, the value "13" falls under the class 10–19.

Therefore, the median class is 10–19.

3.3 General Properties of Measures of the Middle and Measures of Central Tendency

1. The mean is the most unique measure among the measures of the middle, discussed in Section 3.2 above. Unlike the other measures of the middle, the mean is not one of the data values in the dataset. With its uniqueness, the mean is used to compute other statistics, such as variance and standard deviation.

2. The mean is affected the most by the outliers in the dataset. Extremely high and low data values affect the mean adversely. The other measures, such as mode and median, are less affected by outliers since they are drawn from the data values.

3. A dataset may have one mode, two modes, many modes, and sometimes no mode.

4. The mid-range value is also affected by outliers in the dataset.

3.4 Measures of Dispersion

As we have seen previously, measures of central tendency provide insights into the center or middle of a dataset. However, they do not reveal how data points are spread around the center. Measures of dispersion reveal the variability or spread from the mean. They enable business professionals to evaluate risks, compare datasets, and gain deeper insights into data reliability and consistency. These measures include:

1. Range
2. Interquartile range
3. Variance
4. Standard deviation
5. Coefficient of variation

3.4.1 Range

Range is the difference between the maximum and minimum values in a set of numbers. In a dataset, the range is given as:

Range = Maximum value {dataset} – minimum value {dataset}

In business, the range provides a quick sense of variability. For example, in sales data, the range of daily revenue can indicate how much sales fluctuate, helping to identify high-risk days or unexpected outliers.

Example

Calculate the range for the sample of stock prices drawn from the two companies in Table 3.5 below:

Table 3.5	Stock prices drawn from two companies									
Company A	27	25	26	30	35	25	29	30	30	28
Company B	42	38	40	42	41	38	39	40	43	41

Solution

Given the stock prices above, the range of stock prices for both Company A and Company B can be calculated as follows:

Range = Maximum stock price – Minimum stock price

Range for Company A = 35 – 25 = 10

Range for Company B = 43 – 38 = 5

3.4.2 Interquartile range

Quartiles are values that divide datasets into four quarters when the dataset is arranged in ascending order. A dataset will have three quartiles: Q1, Q2, and Q3. Q1 is the first quartile, and 25% of the data values in the dataset are below this value. Q2 is the second quartile, and 50% of data values in the dataset fall below it. Q2 is also the median of the dataset. Q3 is the third quartile, and 75% of the data values fall below it in the dataset.

The advantage of applying and using this measure is that it ignores extreme values in a variable. Business analysts can conduct customer satisfaction surveys without worrying about their Interquartile Range (IQR) values being skewed by a few very high or very low ratings.

Consider the sorted data {2, 2, 4, 5, 5, 5, 8, 9, 9, 9, 12}. The quartiles are as shown below in Figure 3.3.

Figure 3.3 **Quartiles**

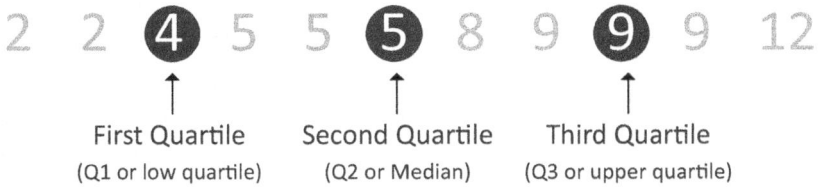

First Quartile	Second Quartile	Third Quartile
(Q1 or low quartile)	(Q2 or Median)	(Q3 or upper quartile)

IQR is the difference between a distribution's third-quartile (Q3) and first-quartile (Q1).

IQR = Q3 – Q1

The Interquartile range for the data given above is: $9 - 4 = 5$.

We can also compute the quartile deviation if the interquartile range is known. The quartile deviation measures the extent to which the upper and lower quartiles deviate from the median value.

Quartile deviation = $\frac{1}{2}(Q3 - Q1)$.

A coefficient of deviation = $\frac{(Q3 - Q1)}{(Q3 + Q1)}$

3.4.3 Variance

Variance measures the spread or variability of the data values from the mean. The symbol for sample variance is s^2 while σ^2 denotes the population variance.

The sample variance of a sample dataset $X = \{x_1, x_2, x_3, x_4, \ldots, x_n\}$ is given by:

$$S^2 = \frac{n\left(\sum_{i=1}^{n}(x_i)^2\right) - \left(\sum_{i=1}^{n}x_i\right)^2}{n(n-1)}, \text{ where } n \text{ is the number of data}$$

values in the dataset X and x_i denotes individual data values in the dataset.

The above formula gives the most accurate value of the sample variance. However, the mean of the sample can also be used in the formula. In that case, the formula is given as:

$$S^2 = \frac{\sum_{i=1}^{n}(x_i - \bar{x})^2}{(n-1)}$$

In the new formula, $\bar{x}$ is the mean of the sample.

For the population variance σ^2, the formula is:

$$\sigma^2 = \frac{\sum_{i=1}^{N}(x_i - \mu)^2}{N}, \text{ where } \mu \text{ is the population mean, and } N$$

total number of items/data values in the population.

Variance is an important measure in business. It is used to evaluate investment return risks, unpredictability of stocks, and how far a business is from its profits or sales targets.

Example

Let us calculate the variance for sample stocks from the two companies whose stock prices are shown in Table 3.6 below:

Table 3.6 — Stock prices drawn from two companies

StatEdge Electronics	27	25	26	30	35	25	29	30	30	28
BizStat Insights	42	38	40	42	41	38	39	40	43	41

Solution

Variance for the stock prices for StatEdge Electronics:

The sample mean stock price for StatEdge Electronics, calculated previously in Example A of Section 3.1, is 28.5 (i.e., $\bar{x} = 28.5$).

Table 3.7 — Squared differences in stock prices: The StatEdge Electronics case

StatEdge Electronics Stock Prices (x)	$x - \bar{x}$	$(x - \bar{x})^2$
27	-1.5	2.25
25	-3.5	12.25
26	-2.5	6.25
30	1.5	2.25
35	6.5	42.25
25	-3.5	12.25
29	0.5	0.25
30	1.5	2.25
30	1.5	2.25
28	-0.5	0.25
Sum	0	82.5

The dispersion of a dataset's actual values relative to its theoretical mean is quantified by its variance. Then, considering the given sample, the standard deviation can be found from the formula of the variance:

$$\text{var(x)} = S^2 = \frac{\sum_{i=1}^{n}(x_i - \bar{x})^2}{(n-1)}$$

$$S^2 = \frac{82.5}{(10-1)} = 9.16667$$

Variance for the stock prices for BizStat Insights:

The sample mean stock price, for BizStat Insights, calculated previously in Example A of Section 3.1, is 40.6 (i.e., $\bar{x}$ = 40.6).

Table 3.8 **Squared differences from sample mean: The BizStat Insights case**

BizStat Insights Stock Prices (x)	$x - \bar{x}$	$(x - \bar{x})^2$
42	1.4	1.96
38	-2.6	6.76
40	-0.6	0.36
42	1.4	1.96
41	0.4	0.16
40	-0.6	0.36
39	-1.6	2.56
40	-0.6	0.36
43	2.4	5.76
41	0.4	0.16
Sum	**0**	**20.4**

The sample variance formula is used since we are dealing with samples of stock prices for the two companies:

$$\text{var(x)} = S^2 = \frac{\sum_{i=1}^{n}\left(x_i - \overline{x}\right)^2}{(n-1)}$$

$$S^2 = \frac{20.4}{(10-1)} = 2.26667$$

The sample variances can also be calculated in Excel using the command below (assuming that the data values are in the range (C6:C15):

= VAR.S(C6:C15)

The range C6:C15 can be substituted with the correct range containing the stock prices.

StatEdge Electronics has a higher variance than BizStat Insights. This implies that the stocks for StatEdge Electronics are more dispersed than the stocks for BizStat Insights. However, in some cases, the variance may not be reasonable.

For instance, in the example above, the variances are in *stocks*^{2} units. This leads to the computation of the standard deviation, the square root of the variance. The standard deviation measure ensures we get a value in the same units as the original data. Let's understand it in the upcoming section.

3.4.4 Standard deviation

The symbol for sample standard deviation is s, while σ denotes the population standard deviation.

The standard deviation is mostly preferred over the variance for the following reasons:

1. The standard deviation has the same units as the original data values, allowing for easier comparison and interpretation.

2. Variance is very sensitive to outlier values in the dataset. Both variance and standard deviation are affected by outliers, but the standard deviation is affected slightly less. Calculating the square root of variance when computing the standard deviation limits reduces the impact of extreme values in the dataset to a certain extent.

To compute the standard deviation of a random variable x, we have the following formula:

Standard deviation: $S_x = \sqrt{var\ (x)}$

We have seen that the sample variance is given by

$$\frac{\sum_{i=1}^{n}(x_i - \bar{x})^2}{(n-1)}$$

Therefore, $s_x = \sqrt{\dfrac{\sum_{i=1}^{n}(x_i - \bar{x})^2}{(n-1)}}$

The standard deviation for StatEdge Electronics and BizStat Insights can be obtained as follows, based on the values from the Variance example above in Section 3.4.3, where the sample variance for StatEdge Electronics is 9.16667 and for BizStat Insights is 2.66667

Standard deviation $S_x = \sqrt{var\ (x)}$

StatEdge Electronics: $S_x = \sqrt{9.16667} = 3.02765$

BizStat Insights: $S_x = \sqrt{2.66667} = 1.505545$

The standard deviation is mostly applicable in production and quality control processes. For instance, a shoe manufacturer can measure various production metrics on manufactured shoes to determine if they are consistent to requirements and accepted standards.

As discussed in this section, the standard deviation is preferred over the variance. However, comparing the dispersion of multiple distributions is sometimes challenging when the units differ. For this reason, the coefficient of variation is introduced.

3.4.5 Coefficient of variation

The Coefficient of Variation (CV) is a statistical measure that is used to measure the spread or variability of data points from the mean by comparing standard deviations. It is usually expressed as a percentage. The coefficient of variation is computed using the formula below:

$$\text{Coefficient of variation (CV)} = \frac{STANDARD\ DEVIATION}{MEAN} * 100$$

$$\text{Sample CV} = \frac{s}{\bar{x}} * 100$$

$$\text{Population CV} = \frac{\sigma}{\mu} * 100 \text{ where } \sigma \text{ is the population}$$

standard deviation and μ is the population mean.

Companies can apply CV when comparing profit margins across regions or product lines to understand where variability is relatively higher.

Example

Peter wants to invest, and he needs to decide between stocks and bonds. Let's assume that stocks have a volatility of 6% with a projected return of 14%, while bonds have a volatility of 4% and a projected return of 16%. Which is the best option for Peter?

Solution

This problem can be solved using the coefficient of variation.

Coefficient of variation (CV) for stocks

$$= \frac{STANDARD\ DEVIATION}{MEAN} * 100$$

We take volatility to be the standard deviation, given that it indicates the spread or variability of stocks from their projected return.

$$= \frac{volatility}{projected\ return} * 100$$

$$= \frac{6}{14} * 100 = 42.857\%$$

Coefficient of variation (CV) for bonds

$$= \frac{STANDARD\ DEVIATION}{MEAN} * 100$$

$$= \frac{volatility}{projected\ return} * 100$$

$$= \frac{4}{16} * 100 = 25\%$$

Peter should invest in bonds as they have a lower risk-to-return ratio than stocks.

In this chapter, we have explored the foundational tools of descriptive statistics, including measures of central tendency, measures of the middle, their general properties, and measures of dispersion. These concepts provide the essential framework for summarizing and interpreting data, enabling professionals to gain meaningful insights into patterns and variability.

By mastering these techniques, you can effectively describe datasets, identify key trends, and make data-driven decisions with confidence. This understanding lays the groundwork for diving into the next chapter on Probability Distributions, where we explore how data behaves under different probabilistic models and extend our analysis to predictive insights.

Chapter Summary

- The three main measures of central tendency are mean, mode, and median.

- The mean is the average of all data points in a dataset obtained by summing all the data values and dividing the sum by the total number of values.

- The most frequent data value in a dataset is known as the mode, while the median is the middle value in a dataset.

- The mean is unique and not necessarily present in the dataset.

- Datasets may have one or multiple modes.

- Outliers can influence the measures of central tendency and dispersion.

- Measures of dispersion measure the spread of a distribution. They include the variance, standard deviation, and coefficient of variation.

- The variance can be used to measure investment risks and unpredictability in stocks.

- Production and quality control processes are measured for consistency by determining the standard deviation of key production metrics.

- The coefficient of variation is preferred over the standard deviation when comparing means with different standard deviations.

Further Learning

(Links also available in Online Resources)

1. **Descriptive statistics**
   http://bit.ly/4fBRHGg

2. **Introduction to descriptive statistics**
   http://bit.ly/47nmNyY

3. **Measures of location**
   http://bit.ly/45uUrR0

4. **Measures of location by Pradnya Ambatipudi**
   http://bit.ly/45ut7SO

5. **Mean, median, & mode - Measures of central tendency**
   http://bit.ly/45VapFf

Quiz

1. **What is the purpose of the mean in descriptive statistics?**
   a. To identify the most frequently occurring value
   b. To measure the spread of data
   c. To represent the average value

2. **If a dataset has outliers, which measure of central tendency is less influenced by extreme values?**
   a. Mean
   b. Median
   c. Range

3. **The range of a dataset is calculated as:**
   a. The difference between the highest and lowest values
   b. The average of all values
   c. The middle value in a sorted dataset

4. **Which of the following statements correctly describes the coefficient of variation?**
   a. It is expressed in the same units as the data.
   b. It is useful for comparing the dispersion of datasets with different units.
   c. It is a measure of central tendency.

5. Ten people were asked about the number of hours they actively do sports per week. For the following data, determine the mode, median, and standard deviation. (Detailed solution included in Online Resources.)

Table 3.9	Hours of exercise per week per person								
Person	1	2	3	4	5	6	7	8	9	10
Hours of exercise per week	23	12	7	7	4	33	12	2	7	3

I. What is the mean number of hours the ten people actively engage in sports?

   a. 11

   b. 9.5

   c. 8.7

II. Calculate the standard deviation of the hours spent on exercises for the ten people.

   a. 9.5

   b. 9.0

   c. 9.8

III. How many hours do most people dedicate to exercise per week?

   a. 7

   b. 8

   c. 23

6. In evaluating an employee, a company assigns 60% weight to project delivery, while teamwork is weighted 40% to make a total of 100 percentage points. An employee of the company scores 4.5 and 4.0 on project delivery and teamwork, respectively. What is the overall performance score for the employee (Hint: Concept of the Weighted Average)?

   a. 4.35
   b. 4.45
   c. 4.30

7. In the stock market, stock X provides a 15% return while stock Y returns 10%. If stock X is weighted 40% while stock Y is weighted 60%, what is the overall return for the two stocks (Hint: Concept of the Weighted Average)?

   a. 12.8%
   b. 12.0%
   c. 12.2%

8. Why is the coefficient of variation useful in comparing two datasets?

   a. It accounts for outliers.
   b. It adjusts for differing units.
   c. It measures central tendency.

9. What does the second quartile represent?

   a. The middle value
   b. The maximum value
   c. The minimum value

10. Which of the following measures is not a measure of dispersion?
    a. Standard deviation
    b. Median
    c. Coefficient of variation

Answers

1 – c	2 – b	3 – a	4 – b	5 – i) a
5 – ii) c	5 – iii) a	6 – c	7 – b	8 – b
9 – a	10 – b			

CHAPTER 4
Probability Distribution

Key Learning Objectives

- Understand random variables.
- Gain insight into probability rules.
- Study discrete distributions.
- Learn continuous distributions.

Building on the knowledge of data collection, presentation, and the measures of central tendency and dispersion discussed previously, we will transition from descriptive statistics to inferential tools in this chapter. Chapter Four introduces the foundational concepts for understanding and modeling uncertainty in business settings through probability distributions. Probability distributions are effective tools for interpreting complex data and directing decision-making in a variety of contexts, including project risk assessment, sales forecasting, and consumer demand estimation.

By linking data characteristics to probability models, this tool provides the framework for predicting outcomes and making informed business decisions based on statistical evidence.

Consider yourself in charge of overseeing the smooth operation of a busy call center as the customer service manager. You become aware that precisely forecasting client wait times is essential for preserving service levels, making the most use of staffing resources, and raising customer satisfaction levels as calls pour in throughout the day.

With variables including call volume, agent availability, and client issues, every call presents a different scenario. You would need knowledge of the probabilistic nature of call arrivals and service times to make accurate wait time predictions. Probability distributions are extremely useful in this situation. You may model the likelihood of various wait time scenarios and make well-informed decisions to increase call center efficiency by using probability distributions.

It is inevitable to experience uncertainty in a dynamic corporate world. Enterprises encounter a wide array of uncertainties that may impact their operations and choices, ranging from inventory control and demand forecasting to evaluating financial hazards and optimizing processes.

In short, probability distributions help firms make sound decisions based on statistical probabilities and comprehend the underlying randomness in a variety of operations. Businesses can detect possible risks and opportunities and obtain a greater understanding of their operations. They are equipped to make strategic decisions to propel success by learning probability distributions.

4.1 Random Variables

In the context of probability distributions, a random variable is referred to as the numerical outcome that arises from a random process or experiment.

Consider an analyst managing a company website with a lot of traffic. The number of customers landing on the website can vary unpredictably based on a number of factors such as marketing strategies, search engine rankings, as well as competition from websites with similar keywords. This scenario presents a perfect random variable case as the number of persons visiting the website can be counted, and the numerical outcome can be recorded.

Random variables are of two types: discrete and continuous variables. They are explained as follows:

1. Discrete random variables

A discrete random variable is one that can take on a countable number of distinct values. These values are typically integers or whole numbers, and each one corresponds to a specific probability.

Examples:

- The number of customers visiting a business webpage in a day
- The number of deformed products in a batch
- The number of successful recruits on an insurance scheme in a month

2. Continuous random variable

A continuous variable is a random variable that can take an infinite number of values within a specified range. Continuous random variables are an uncountable set and can include decimals and fractions. We can also say that continuous variables form a continuum. For instance, the measurement of a product's weight between 140 and 141 kg could fall on any indefinite value in that range, including values with decimals.

Examples:

- The waiting time for a customer on a service call
- The length, weight, and height of a product from a production process
- Operating temperature in a milk cooling plant

Having studied the distinct types of random variables evaluated in probability distributions, let us explore the rules of probability in the upcoming section.

4.2 Probability Rules

As discussed in Chapter One, Section 1.5, probability is the likelihood or chance of an event happening. Probability can also determine the "odds" that an event will happen. Businesses can apply probability in their daily operations to predict the likelihood or odds of events occurring.

For example, the odds of customers defaulting on their loans could be estimated and used to determine loan amounts in a micro-finance institution. Similarly, a manufacturing plant may predict the number of products likely to be defective based on its production records.

- A probability experiment is defined by chance, leading to specific outcomes known as events.

- An event is the result of a single trial of an experiment.

- All possible outcomes of an experiment form the sample space. Therefore, events are subsets of the sample space.

Let's consider the following scenario to illustrate these terms.

Production managers in a lithium battery manufacturing company are likely to use hypothesis testing to evaluate an assertion. They aim to test whether the electrolyte levels in lithium-ion batteries produced make up 16% of the battery cells before they are released to the market. The manager wishes to gather data from the production line and as such, he chooses 100 batteries at random to be tested.

- **Probability experiment:** The manager is interested in testing the electrolyte level of the batteries manufactured in the company. Each tested battery could either have an electrolyte level that is 16% of the cell or different from 16%. These are the outcomes for the probability experiment.

- **Sample space:** The sample space for this experiment consists of all possible outcomes for each battery. In this case, the sample space is "electrolyte level makes up 16% of the cell, or electrolyte level does not make up 16% of the cell."

- **Event:** In this context, an event refers to a situation where a battery does not contain electrolyte at the level constituting 16% of the cell. For instance, the event "more than 10% of the tested batteries had electrolyte levels differing from 16% of the cell" comprises instances where the number of batteries with electrolyte levels which does not equal 16% of the cell exceeds 10% of the total number of tested batteries.

4.2.1 Defining probability rules from the lithium-ion battery example:

Let's understand probability rules using the above example:

1. **Probability of an event**

   To be more precise, let an event be said to be represented by the symbol E. Then, the probability of an event occurring, stated as P(E), represents the likelihood of that event taking place. The probability, P(E), is an uncertain or stochastic value that can be a rationalized fraction or decimal lying between zero and one.

   For a tested battery in the given example, the chance of having an electrolyte level that was not 16% of the cell would be represented as P(electrolyte level different from 16% of the cell) = 0.15.

   A probability of 0.15 can be written in a verbal form to mean that there is a 15% probability or chance that a battery tested will show deviation in the electrolyte level from 16% of the cell.

2. **Impossibility of an event**

   In a probability experiment, there exists a notion that if an event can never occur, then the probability of the occurrence of that event is zero. In the given example, this event is realized when each of the tested batteries is found to have an electrolyte level that is equal to 16% of the cell such that the probability of electrolyte levels differing from 16% of the cell P(E) is 0.

3. Certainty of an event

This kind of event in the probability experiment is considered certain to occur, and such an event is usually called a certain event. In this case, where an event is certain to happen, the probability of the event is denoted as $P(E) = 1$.

So, in the example above, if all the batteries in the sample of 100 batteries have an electrolyte level not equal to 16% of the cell, then the probability of the lithium-ion batteries having electrolyte levels not equal to 16% of the cell is 1.

4. Sum of probabilities

Another feature related to probability is that the probabilities of all the events or outcomes in a probability experiment must sum up to 1. In the above example, our successful outcome is a battery whose electrolyte level is 16% of the cell. An unsuccessful outcome is a battery that has a different level of electrolyte than 16% of the cell. The sum of the probability of successful outcomes and the probability of unsuccessful outcomes should equal 1.

5. Complement of an event

The complement of event E is denoted as $\overline{E}$ and contains all outcomes in the sample space that are not included in event E. Therefore, we have $P(\overline{E}) = 1 - P(E)$.

In the example of electrolyte levels, if it is determined that the probability for a tested battery to have an electrolyte level of 16% of the cell is 0.80, then the probability of the complement can be calculated as follows:

$$P(\overline{E}) = 1 - P(E)$$
$$P(\overline{E}) = 1 - 0.80 = 0.20$$

The probability of the complement, $P(\overline{E})$, obtained in this case, represents the probability of a tested battery having an electrolyte level different from 16% of the cell.

4.2.2 Additional rules for probability

We will understand additional rules for probability based on the occurrence of "mutually exclusive scenarios" in the following example.

Let us imagine two discrete events that cannot overlap, and let them be, for instance, event A and event B. With regards to probability studies, the events A and B are usually understood to be mutually exclusive. To put this in context, a businessman can only make a profit or loss after selling a product. Making a profit or a loss cannot occur to the businessman at the same time while selling his product.

Consider the following example:

1. **Choice of buying an apartment:** Lucy is deciding between purchasing an apartment in Texas and Miami.
    The events "Purchase an apartment in Texas" and "Purchase an apartment in Miami" are mutually exclusive events since Lucy has to decide and make a final choice between the two locations. Choosing to purchase the apartment in Texas precludes Lucy from purchasing an apartment in Miami.

2. **Payment choices:** Suppose Lucy makes up her mind and decides to purchase an apartment in Miami, where she is offered to pay in cash or using a credit card. She will also have to select her preferred choice of payment and forego the other choice. The payment choices are also mutually exclusive.

The following are the additional rules for probability in this context:

1. If A and B are mutually exclusive, the probability P(A or B) can be expressed as P(A) + P(B).

2. If it is known that A and B are not mutually exclusive, the probability P(A or B) can be expressed as P(A) + P(B) − P(A and B).

Suppose a garment-making factory has 1000 employees who are distributed across different departments as follows:

A. Finance department: 400 workers

B. Human resources department: 300 workers

C. Marketing department: 300 workers

The probability of selecting a random worker who is either from the marketing or finance department is:

$$P(C \text{ or } A) = \frac{300}{1000} + \frac{400}{1000} = \frac{700}{1000} = 0.7$$

4.2.3 Multiplication rules and conditional probability

Two events are said to be independent if the occurrence of one event A does not depend on the occurrence of the other event B. If two events A and B are not independent, then they are dependent and a conditional probability $P(B|A)$ can be calculated. The $P(B|A)$ is the probability of an event B happening given that event A has already happened.

$$P(B|A) = \frac{P(A \text{ and } B)}{P(A)} = \frac{P(A \cap B)}{P(A)}$$

Multiplication rules for probability:

1. The probability P(A and B) = P(A) and P(B) if A and B are independent events.

2. The probability P(A and B) = P(A) and P(B|A) if A and B are dependent events.

Assume there is a restaurant which offers an opportunity to some customers to give their feedback on the received service before they leave. The restaurant seeks to find out how many people give a positive reaction to the service they received from the restaurant. According to the restaurant survey, the probability of a customer being satisfied is 0.7, while the probability that a customer is satisfied and leaves a positive review is 0.6. Calculate the probability of a customer leaving a positive review provided that she is satisfied.

$$P(\text{Positive} \mid \text{Satisfied}) = \frac{P(\text{Satisfied and Positive})}{P(\text{Satisfied})}$$

$P(\text{Positive and Satisfied}) = 0.6$

$$P(\text{Positive} \mid \text{Satisfied}) = \frac{0.6}{0.7}$$

$P(\text{Positive} \mid \text{Satisfied}) = 0.857$

The probability, P(Positive | Satisfied), is 0.857 and indicates that if a customer is satisfied, the probability of her giving a positive review is 0.857.

4.2.4 Classical probability

In classical probability, probability is calculated based on the sample spaces. It is assumed that every outcome in the sample space has an equal chance of occurring.

Suppose a probability experiment has an Event E, the probability of E is P(E), n(E) is the number of n outcomes of the event E, while n(S) is the total number of all possible outcomes in the sample space S.

We can calculate P(E) as follows:

$$P(E) = \frac{n(E)}{n(S)}$$

4.2.5 Empirical probability

Empirical probability is the estimation of the likelihood of an event happening based on its past data or observed frequencies. Unlike classical probability that assumes that every outcome in the sample space has an equal chance of happening, there must be a record of past occurrences to estimate empirical probability. Empirical probability can also be known as experimental probability.

Suppose an insurance seller plans to predict the probability of customers buying insurance after they have had an insurance campaign in their company. In order to calculate the empirical probability, the seller should collect data on the number of customers who were exposed to the marketing campaign and the number of customers who actually bought the insurance after the campaign was launched.

The probability of successful insurance purchases is given as the number of successful purchases divided by the number of customers who were targeted during the campaign (the denominator).

Assume that the total consumers who came across the campaign is 200 and, out of that, 40 took the insurance. Empirical probability is the chance of occurrence of an event in any given sample selected from a larger population. The empirical probability of a successful insurance purchase after the campaign can be estimated as below.

Using empirical probability:
- Number of customers that purchased insurance = 40
- Total number of customers reached through the marketing campaign = 200

P (Purchasing insurance) =

$$\frac{\textit{Number of customers that purchased insurance}}{\textit{Total number of customers reached through the campaign}}$$

P (Purchasing insurance) = $\dfrac{40}{200}$ = 0.2

20% of customers are likely to purchase insurance after a marketing campaign.

4.3 Discrete Probability Distributions

A discrete probability distribution is a probability function of the likelihood of occurrence of each possible outcome of a discrete random variable. As discussed in Section 4.1, discrete random variables have a countable image set: for instance, the total sales made in a day, the number of customers served in a restaurant, and the number of employees that were reported late to work.

4.3.1 Conditions for a discrete probability function

A function $f(x)$ is said to follow a discrete probability distribution if x is a random variable with values x1, x2, x3, x4, ..., $f(x)$ and x meets the following conditions:

1. The probability of each outcome is a positive numerical value in the range of 0 and 1 expressed as: $0 \leq f(x) \leq 1$.

2. The sum of all possible outcomes is 1, mathematically expressed as:

$$\sum_{i=1}^{n} f(xi) = 1 \text{ where } i = 1,2,3,\ldots.,n$$

and

$$\sum_{i=1}^{\infty} f(xi) = 1 \text{ where } i = 1,2,3,4,\ldots \text{ to infinity}$$

4.3.2 Types of discrete probability distributions

Understanding probability distributions is essential for making informed business decisions, as they help quantify uncertainty and predict outcomes. In this section, we focus on discrete probability distributions, which are particularly useful for analyzing situations like sales forecasts, customer arrivals, or quality control defects. By exploring key distributions such as the Binomial, Poisson, and Geometric distributions, professionals can apply these tools to solve practical problems and optimize decision-making processes.

The words "success" and "failure" are commonly used in probability distributions. However, it should be known that "success" does not refer to a favorable outcome but rather the outcome of interest, while "failure" implies failing to observe the outcome of interest.

1. **Discrete uniform distribution**

   A discrete uniform distribution can be defined as a distribution whereby all the outcomes that make up the sample space are assumed to have an equal probability of occurrence. Examples are: having to select an egg from a tray at a given instance at random without any fixed or predetermined sequence. Another example is tossing a die in such a way that each face of the die has an equal probability of showing up.

2. Bernoulli distribution

A Bernoulli probability distribution describes an experiment where exactly one trial is being conducted, and the possible results are binary in nature. Examples of Bernoulli distribution experiments include flipping a coin (the outcomes are Head and Tail), rolling a die once to get a specific outcome (e.g., rolling a 2; the outcome is either a 2 or any other number on the die [i.e., 1, 3,4,5, and 6]), a customer making a decision on whether to purchase a product (the customer may purchase or fail to purchase the product).

3. Binomial distribution

A Binomial distribution extends the Bernoulli distribution by modeling the number of successes in a fixed number of independent trials of a Bernoulli experiment. In order to understand how a binomial distribution works, let's consider the following example of a Bernoulli distribution first and see how it gives rise to the Binomial type of distribution.

Suppose that a coin is tossed once and the possible outcomes are HEAD or TAIL. Such an experiment with only two outcomes is referred to as a Bernoulli distribution whose probability mass function is given by:

$f(x) = p^x q^{1-x}$ *for x = 0, 1, where p is the probability of success, q is the probability of failure, and x represents the number of successes.*

Suppose the experiment is repeated n times, such that we are interested in x successes in n trials, then it means that we will have x successes and $(n-x)$ failures. This is a binomial distribution.

Therefore, we can redefine a binomial distribution such that x is said to follow a binomial distribution with a probability mass function:

$$f(X) = \binom{n}{k} p^x q^{n-x}$$

mean: $\mu = E[X] = np$

variance : $var(x) = \sigma^2 = npq$

where n: total number of trials

      x: total number of successes in a single trial

      p: probability of success in a single trial

      q: probability of failure in a single trial

In summary, a distribution is considered binomial if:

- There are only two possible outcomes in each trial.
- The probability of success (or failure) remains constant throughout all the trials.
- The outcomes of different trials are independent.

Example A

A textile factory receives an order from a client to manufacture 50 men's suits for a wedding. Records at the factory show that 5% of suits from past orders turned out to be unsatisfactory and did not meet client specifications. What is the probability that exactly 3 suits from the new order will turn out to be unsatisfactory to the client?

Solution:

The formula to be used is: $f(X) = \binom{n}{k} p^x q^{n-x}$

$n = 50$ (number of suits ordered)

$p = 0.05$ (probability that a suit will not meet the client specification)

$x = 3$ (number of defective components)

$q = 1 - p = 1 - 0.05 = 0.95$ (the probability that a suit will meet client specification)

$$f(X = x) = \binom{50}{3} 0.05^3 0.95^{50-3}$$

In the formula above:

A. X represents the number of unsatisfactory suits in the order of 50

B. x represents the specific number of successes. Thus, $x = 3$ means we are interested in the probability that exactly 3 suits turn out unsatisfactory.

Probability of exactly 3 suits from the new order turning out to be unsatisfactory to the client:

The formula to be used is: $f(X) = \binom{n}{k} p^x q^{n-x}$

Where $\binom{n}{k}$ also ${}_nC_k$ is $\dfrac{n!}{(n-k)!k!}$

Therefore,

$$P(X = 3) = \binom{50}{3} 0.05^3 0.95^{50-3}$$

$$P(X = 3) = \frac{50!}{3!(50-3)!} (0.05)^3 (0.95)^{47}$$

$P(X = 3) = 0.21987$

Therefore, the probability that exactly 3 components are defective is approximately 21.987%.

Example B

An insurance seller is assured of a 20% chance of selling car insurance any time he makes a call to prospective clients. On a certain day, the seller makes 50 calls to prospective clients. What is the probability that the seller will sell fewer than 10 car insurance policies on that day?

Solution:

$n = 50$ (number of sales calls)

$p = 0.20$ (probability of success in closing a deal)

$x = 0, 1, 2, ..., 9$ (fewer than 10 closed deals)

$q = 1 - p = 1 - 0.20 = 0.80$ (probability that the seller will not sell any car insurance)

We need to find the cumulative probability from 0 to 9.

Using the binomial cumulative probability formula:

$$P(X < 10) = \sum_{x=0}^{9} \binom{n}{k} p^x q^{n-x}$$

This calculation involves summing up the individual probabilities from $x = 0$ to $x = 9$.

Use the Binomial Probability Distribution Calculator to obtain the probabilities from 0 to 9 as shown below. This calculator is also available in the Excel template "Chapter 4_Discrete_Probability_Distributions," part of the Online Resources of the book.

The URL to access the same has been added at the end of the book in the "Statistical Tables" section, and can be accessed through Online Resources.

Figure 4.1 The probability distribution in Excel

n		50		E(x) = μ	10.00
p		0.2		Var(x) = σ²	8
				Std dev = σ	2.83

x	P(X = x)	P(X <= x)
0	0.0000	0.0000
1	0.0002	0.0002
2	0.0011	0.0013
3	0.0044	0.0057
4	0.0128	0.0185
5	0.0295	0.0480
6	0.0554	0.1034
7	0.0870	0.1904
8	0.1169	0.3073
9	0.1364	0.4437
10	0.1398	0.5836
11	0.1271	0.7107

Discrete Probability General   Binomial Probability Distrib.   Poisson Probability Distrib.

The probability for P(X <= 9) = 0.4437

4. Geometric probability distribution

A geometric probability distribution is used to determine the probability of success after an independent number of trials. Each trial must have two outcomes.

Example A

A company is rolling out a sales discount campaign on its e-commerce website. The discount will apply to lucky customers only. Suppose we want to determine the number of purchases to be made before a customer gets the discount.

We will need to apply a geometric probability distribution to assess the distribution of the number of purchases made before the sales discount applies to a customer (success).

The geometric distribution is $P(X = x) = p \cdot q^{(x-1)}$, $x = 1, 2, 3, \ldots$, where x is the number of trials until the first success, for which probability is being sought. In this case, p is the probability of a success for a single trial, and $q = 1 - p$ is the probability of a failure for a single trial.

Example B

It is a policy in Mark's factory that all iron sheets must undergo quality checks before dispatch. On average, 1 in 20 iron sheets are defective. What is the probability that exactly 3 iron sheets will be inspected before a defective iron sheet can be found?

Solution

1 in 20 iron sheets are defective (this is 0.05 as a probability).

$p = 0.05$ (probability of defect)

$n = 3$ (number of trials until success)

$q = 1 - p$ = probability that iron sheets are not defective

X = Number of checks before a defective iron sheet is discovered

$P(X = x) = p * q^{(x-1)}$, $x = 1, 2, 3, \ldots$ where x is the number of trials until the first success

$P(X = 3) = 0.05 * 0.95^{(3-1)} = 0.045125$

Therefore, the probability that exactly 3 iron sheets will be inspected before finding the first defective one is 4.5125%.

Example C

A Telco company based in Texas receives heavy traffic on its customer service lines in an hour. The company hires a number of customer service agents and expects that it will reduce customer wait time to exactly 2 minutes. The company discovers that 20% of the time, technical issues prolong the wait time to 5 minutes. What is the probability that the first call with a 5-minute wait occurs on the 5th call?

Solution

$p = 0.20$ (probability of longer wait time)

$n = 5$ (number of trials until success)

$q = 1 - p$ which is $1 - 0.20 = 0.80$

$P(X = x) = p * q^{(x-1)}$, $x = 1, 2, 3, \ldots$ where x is the number of trials until the first success

$P(X = 5) = 0.20 * 0.80^{(5-1)} = 0.08192$

Therefore, the probability of the next call requiring longer than the average wait time occurring on the 5th call is 8.192%.

Example D

A software developer is certain that the chances of a customer upgrading to a premium version of his software are 10% after expiry of the free trial. What is the probability that the software developer will have to wait for exactly 4 customers to use the free trial version before one customer upgrades to a premium version?

Solution

$p = 0.10$ (probability of success, i.e., upgrade to premium)

$n = 4$ (number of trials until success)

$q = 1 - p = 0.90$ (probability that a customer will not upgrade to premium)

$P(X = x) = p * q^{(x-1)}$, x = 1, 2, 3, ... where x is the number of trials until the first success

$P(X = 4) = 0.10 * 0.90^{(4-1)} = 0.0729$

Therefore, the probability of needing exactly 4 customers before the first conversion occurs is 0.0729 or 7.29%.

5. Poisson distribution

A Poisson probability distribution is used to determine the probability that a certain number of events will happen within a specified period. The rate of occurrence should be determined and remain constant within the specified period. A discrete random variable is a Poisson distribution if its probability mass function is given as:

$$f(x) = \frac{\lambda^x e^{-\lambda}}{x!}$$ for x = 0, 1, 2, 3, ..., n; where n is the total number of trials.

λ is the rate of occurrence; x is the number of successes in n trials.

To calculate the probability of a certain number of events occurring within a fixed interval, the formula below is used:

$$P(X = x) = \frac{\lambda^x e^{-\lambda}}{x!}$$

Where:

A. X is a random variable that represents the number of successes in an experiment. It is a general notation for the outcome of a random process.

B. x is a specific value of the random variable X or a particular realization of the random variable X.

If p (probability of observing a specific number of successes in a given interval) is known from the formula above, then the mean and variance of the Poisson distribution can be calculated as shown below. However, it should be known that the mean and variance in a Poisson distribution are equal to the parameter λ (lambda), which represents the rate of occurrence.

mean of x: $\mu = E[X] = np = \lambda$

variance of x: $var(x) = \lambda$

where n is the total number of trials, x number of successes in the n trials, λ is the rate parameter, and p is the probability of observing a specific number of successes in a given interval.

Example A

A supermarket expects to receive an average of 6 customer complaints per day.

A. Write a mathematical statement for this probability problem.

B. What is the probability of the supermarket receiving fewer than 6 complaints on a given day?

Hint: Of interest is the number of complaints the supermarket receives in a day, therefore, the time interval in this case is one day.

Solution:

Let X be the number of complaints received by the supermarket in a day. If the supermarket expects to receive 6 complaints in a day, then the average is 6 complaints per day.

Mean: 6 customer complaints per day

Mathematical statement for the probability of receiving 6 customer complaints in a day:

$$P(X = 6) = \frac{6^x e^{-6}}{x!}$$

To know the probability of receiving fewer than 6 customer complaints in a day, we need to calculate the probability $P(X \le 6)$:

$$P(X = 0) = \frac{6^0 e^{-6}}{0!} = 0.0025$$

$$P(X = 1) = \frac{6^1 e^{-6}}{1!} = 0.0149$$

$$P(X = 2) = \frac{6^2 e^{-6}}{2!} = 0.0446$$

$$P(X = 3) = \frac{6^3 e^{-6}}{3!} = 0.0892$$

$$P(X = 4) = \frac{6^4 e^{-6}}{4!} = 0.1339$$

$$P(X = 5) = \frac{6^5 e^{-6}}{5!} = 0.1606$$

$$P(X \le 6) = \sum_{x=0}^{6} \left(\frac{6^x e^{-6}}{x!} \right) = 0.0025 + 0.0149 + 0.0446 + 0.0892 + 0.1339 + 0.1606$$

$$P(X \le 6) = 0.4457$$

Example B

It is known that 4% of the items coming out of a production process are deformed. Determine the probability that among 250 items randomly selected from the production process:

a. Exactly 5 are deformed

b. At least 5 are deformed

Solution:

From the problem above, we can calculate the mean as:

mean of x: $\mu = np = \lambda$; $n = 250$, $p = 4\%$ or 0.04

$$\mu = 250*0.04 = 10$$

The probability that exactly 5 are deformed:

$$P(X = 5) = \frac{\lambda^x e^{-\lambda}}{x!} = \frac{10^5 e^{-10}}{5!} = 0.037833$$

Probability that at least 5 are deformed:

$$P(X \geq 5) = 1 - P(X \leq 4)$$

We will need to calculate all the probabilities for $X \leq 4$, then subtract from 1:

$$P(X = 0) = \frac{\lambda^x e^{-\lambda}}{x!} = \frac{10^0 e^{-10}}{0!} = 0.000045$$

$$P(X = 1) = \frac{\lambda^x e^{-\lambda}}{x!} = \frac{10^1 e^{-10}}{1!} = 0.000453$$

$$P(X = 2) = \frac{\lambda^x e^{-\lambda}}{x!} = \frac{10^2 e^{-10}}{2!} = 0.00226$$

$$P(X = 3) = \frac{\lambda^x e^{-\lambda}}{x!} = \frac{10^3 e^{-10}}{3!} = 0.007566$$

$$P(X = 4) = \frac{\lambda^x e^{-\lambda}}{x!} = \frac{10^4 e^{-10}}{4!} = 0.018916$$

$$P(X \leq 4) = 0.000045 + 0.000453 + 0.00226 + 0.007566 + 0.018916 = 0.029252$$

$$P(X \geq 5) = 1 - P(X \leq 4)$$

$$P(X \geq 5) = 1 - 0.029252$$

$$P(X \geq 5) = 0.970748$$

Therefore, the probability that at least 5 are deformed is 0.970748

The probabilities can be obtained using the Poisson Probability Distribution Calculator by entering the correct mean and time /space/intervals or trials. This calculator is also available in the Excel template "Chapter 4_Discrete_Probability_Distributions," part of the Online Resources of the book.

The URL to access the same has been added at the end of the book in the "Statistical Tables" section, and can be accessed through Online Resources.

6. Hypergeometric distribution

A hypergeometric probability distribution determines the likelihood of getting a certain number of successes in draws from a finite population without replacement. Each time an item is drawn, the population decreases and thereby changes the probabilities of obtaining success.

In Excel, the command below is used to calculate probabilities using the hypergeometric distribution.

HYPGEOM.DIST(x, n, k, m, cum)

Where x is the number of successes, n is the sample size, m is the population size, and k is the number of successes in m, while cum is set to FALSE.

Example: Lucy and Natalie are fruit vendors in the same town, but do not know each other. Each of them has about 200 customers in the town. Assume that 200 customers for each vendor represent a random sample from 50,000 people who live in the town. Determine the probability that Lucy and Natalie share a customer.

Excluding Lucy and Natalie from the number of people who live in the town leaves 49,998 people, out of which the 2 groups of customers fall.

We need to calculate the probability that from 200 randomly selected people, none of them will be a customer of the two vendors as follows (using the Excel command below):

HYPGEOM.DIST(0, 200, 200, 49998, FALSE) = 0.448

The probability that a randomly selected person from the 200 is Lucy and Natalie's customer is

$1 - 0.448 = 0.552$ or 55.2%.

There is a 55.2% chance that Lucy and Natalie will share a customer.

4.4 Continuous Probability Distributions

In business, the many factors that we measure, such as delivery times, customer wait times, product weights, daily stock price fluctuations, length of tenure of a CEO, price of a commodity, or even age of an employee, are all continuous in nature.

A continuous probability distribution helps describe the likelihood of different outcomes for these variables within a given range. Understanding these distributions enables professionals to analyze patterns, predict outcomes, and make informed decisions based on data-driven insights.

4.4.1 Conditions for a continuous probability distribution

A probability function $f(x)$ is said to follow a continuous probability distribution if the following conditions are satisfied:

1. The probability of obtaining f(x) is contained in the range 0 and 1, that is, $0 \le f(x) \le 1$ (0 and 1 inclusive)

2. The integration of f(x) gives 1; $\int_0^\infty f(x)dx = 1$ for $0 \le x \le \infty$

Mean and variance of a continuous random variable x:

1. Mean: $\mu = E(X) = \int_0^\infty xf(x)dx$ for $0 \le x \le \infty$

$$= \int_a^b xf(x)dx \text{ for } a \le x \le b$$

2. Variance of x

$$\text{Var}(x) = E(X^2) - \mu^2 = E(X^2) - [E(X)]^2$$

$$= \int_a^b x^2 f(x)dx - \mu^2 \text{ for } a \le x \le b$$

The probabilities of a continuous random variable x are defined as:

$$P(X = x) = \int_{x-\frac{1}{2}}^{x+\frac{1}{2}} f(x)dx$$

$$P(X \le x) = \int_0^x f(x)dx$$

$$P(X \ge x) = \int_x^\infty f(x)dx$$

$$P(a \le x \le b) = \int_a^b f(x)dx$$

4.4.2 The normal probability distribution

Many natural events, when observed over a long time, can be seen to follow a continuous probability distribution. One of the most common continuous distributions observed in nature is the normal distribution. This is often represented by a bell-shaped curve known as the normal distribution curve. For this reason, the normal distribution is commonly used in mathematics and helps solve various ongoing problems.

Mean and standard deviation are the parameters used to describe the shape of a normal curve. The mean, denoted by μ, represents the center of a distribution, and the standard deviation, represented by σ, shows how spread out or compact a distribution is from the middle point.

On a standard normal distribution, 68.27% of values usually lie within one standard deviation of the mean, while 95.4% of values lie within two standard deviations. 99.73% of all values in the distribution lie within three standard deviations of the mean. This can be demonstrated as below.

Imagine a company whose average employee age is 40 years with a standard deviation of 4 years. Using the standard normal distribution, 68.27% of the ages of the employees can be predicted to fall between 35 and 45 years (within one standard deviation), 95.4% of employee ages to fall between 30 and 50 years (within two standard deviations), while 99.73% of employees ages fall between 25 and 55 years (within three standard deviations).

Figure 4.2 **The normal distribution curve**

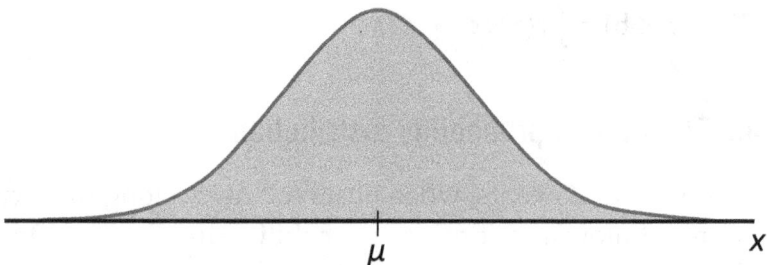

Characteristics of a normal distribution curve:

- It is bell-shaped
- The total area under the curve is equal to 1
- The three measures of central tendency all lie along the line of symmetry
- It is symmetrical around the mean μ

On the normal distribution curve, the values of the random variable x are absolute in terms of units and magnitude. This means a specific normal distribution cannot be directly applied to datasets with different ranges or scales of x.

To address this problem, the normal distribution curve is standardized by converting the horizontal scale into a standardized scale. The standardized scale measures the distance in standard deviations by which a random variable x is away from the mean μ.

The standardized random variable x becomes z given as:

$z = \dfrac{x-\mu}{\sigma}$ where x is the original value on the horizontal scale, and z is the standardized value of x measured in standard deviations.

In the standardized normal distribution, the probability density function (p.d.f) of the continuous variable z is given by:

$$f(z) = \frac{1}{\sqrt{2\pi}} e^{-\left(\frac{1}{2}\right)z^2} \text{ for } -\infty \leq z \leq \infty, \text{ where } \mu = 0 \text{ and } \sigma = 1.$$

Therefore, $Z \sim N(0, 1)$

Figure 4.3 Standardized normal distribution curve

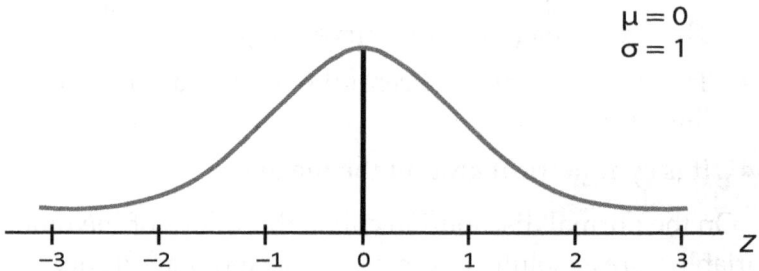

$\mu = 0$
$\sigma = 1$

Understanding key distributions such as the Bernoulli, Binomial, and Normal distributions provides valuable insights into predicting outcomes and assessing risks. This enables professionals to make informed decisions based on probability.

Building on this foundation, the next chapter, Probability and Counting Rules, will deepen our understanding of probability by introducing principles of counting and combinatorics. This will provide us with tools to analyze complex probability problems with efficiency and precision.

Chapter Summary

- Probability distributions are essential for managing and quantifying uncertainty and predicting outcomes in situations involving randomness.

- Random variables represent numerical outcomes from random processes.

- There are two types of random variables: discrete and continuous. Discrete variables are countable, distinct values, often in separate outcomes, while continuous variables take any value within a range, including decimals and fractions.

- Two events cannot happen at the same time if they are mutually exclusive.

- If A and B are mutually exclusive, the probability P(A or B) can be expressed as P(A) + P(B).

- If it is known that A and B are not mutually exclusive, the probability P(A or B) can be expressed as P(A) + P(B) − P(A and B).

- A discrete probability distribution refers to the probability that expresses the likelihood of the occurrence of each possible value of the discrete random variable.

- Continuous probability distributions give the probability that a continuous random variable lies within a specified range.

- The normal distribution curve is usually bell-shaped. The total area under the curve is equal to 1, and it is also symmetrical around the mean μ.

Further Learning

(Links also available in Online Resources)

1. **Random variables and probability distributions**
   http://bit.ly/47y99ZZ

2. **Binomial distributions**
   http://bit.ly/47BlmMp

3. **Poisson distributions**
   http://bit.ly/45mQjUk

4. **Hypergeometric distributions**
   http://bit.ly/3Jk6zgl

Quiz

1. **What is an event in probability?**
   a. Each outcome is in the sample space.
   b. It is a favorable outcome in a probability experiment.
   c. The result of a single trial of an experiment.

2. **Which of the following are the two types of random variables?**
   a. Discrete and Bernoulli
   b. Continuous and deterministic
   c. Continuous and discrete

3. **In probability theory, what does $P(\bar{E})$ represent?**
   a. Probability of event E
   b. Probability of the complement of event E
   c. Probability of event E and event $\bar{E}$ occurring together

4. **In a probability experiment there may be an event which is sure to take place, and, on the other hand, there may be an event which is sure not to take place. What is the likelihood of an occurrence that is bound to occur?**
   a. 0.5
   b. 0
   c. 1

5. One of the following events represents a mutually exclusive event. Which one is it?
   a. Rolling a dice and getting an even number
   b. Flipping a coin and getting a head
   c. Selecting a red card and a black card from a deck of cards

6. Which probability distribution is used to determine the probability of success after k independent trials?
   a. Binomial distribution
   b. Poisson distribution
   c. Geometric distribution

7. The normal distribution curve is characterized by all of the following except?
   a. The normal distribution is always positively skewed.
   b. It is bell-shaped.
   c. The total area under the curve is equal to 1.

8. Which distribution is described by the characteristics below?
   • There are only two possible outcomes in each trial.
   • The probability of success (or failure) remains constant throughout all the trials.
   • The outcomes of different trials are independent.
      a. Normal distribution
      b. Bernoulli distribution
      c. Binomial distribution

9. **Bernoulli and binomial probability distributions are two related distributions. What is the primary difference between these two probability distributions?**
   a. Bernoulli distribution applies to a single trial, while the binomial distribution applies to repeated independent trials.
   b. Bernoulli distribution applies to trials with more than two outcomes, while a binomial distribution applies to trials with only two outcomes.
   c. Bernoulli distributions arise from binomial distributions.

10. **How can the probability of an outcome falling within a specified range be expressed if it follows a continuous probability distribution?**
    a. $P(X = x)$
    b. $P(X \leq x)$
    c. $P(a \leq X \leq b)$

Answers				
1 – c	2 – c	3 – b	4 – c	5 – c
6 – c	7 – a	8 – c	9 – a	10 – c

CHAPTER 5

Probability and Counting Rules

Key Learning Objectives

- Understand counting rules with detailed scenario examples.
- Learn about combining probability and counting rules.

This chapter explores essential counting rules and demonstrates how to combine them with probability to solve practical business problems. By mastering these concepts, professionals and businesses will be empowered to analyze uncertainties and optimize resources. They can thus steer their organizations toward sustained growth and long-term success.

5.1 Counting Rules

Amid the fast-paced currents of the business world, decision-making often involves understanding the likelihood of events. It also requires evaluating the possible outcomes of complex scenarios. Probability provides a framework to quantify uncertainty, while counting rules simplify how we determine possible combinations or arrangements in a situation.

For instance, a product manager might calculate the probability of selecting a winning design from multiple prototypes, or a supply chain analyst might use counting rules to evaluate different logistics arrangements.

In this chapter, we will discuss the following four counting rules:

1. Multiplication of choices rule
2. Combination rule
3. Permutation rule
4. Multiplication of combinations

Before we dive into the different types of counting rules, let's first understand the concept of factorials. Factorials play a fundamental role in counting and probability. They form the basis for understanding permutations and combinations.

Factorial, as used in business, is the methodical listing and combining of every event or result that could occur in a particular situation. It is an essential tool for examining how different aspects or variables are combined or permuted in relation to one another when it comes to decision-making, strategic planning and processing.

Factorial computations, for instance, can be used to determine the many ways in which products can be stacked on a shelf, how staff shifts can be planned out, or how the various feature combinations in a product portfolio can be analyzed. Basically, factorials help businesses measure how complicated a scenario is, equip them to allocate resources as efficiently as possible, and make decisions based on a thorough knowledge of all possible outcomes.

A factorial of k, denoted $k!$ is the product of k with all the positive integers below k, expressed as follows:

$$k! = k(k-1)\ (k-2)\ (k-3),\ \ldots\ldots\ldots\ldots,\ 3,\ 2,\ 1$$

The factorial of 1 is 1, and factorials in fractions can cancel out as shown below:

$$\frac{6!}{4!} = \frac{6^*5^*4^*3^*2^*1}{4^*3^*2^*1} = 6*5 = 30$$

Let's understand each of the counting rules with the help of case scenarios in the following section:

1. Multiplication of choices rule

The multiplication of choices counting rule is a fundamental principle in business statistics. It allows for the systematic calculation of the total number of outcomes in multi-stage events. This rule states that if there are $k1$ ways to make a first choice and $k2$ ways to make a second choice, then there are $k1 \times k2$ total outcomes when both choices are made sequentially.

Multiplication of choices can be applied in business problems where decisions have to be made at multiple stages of a process. Each stage should have its own set of options. For instance, in the production of flavored drinks, the multiplication of choices could be used to determine the possible number of variations.

These variations could involve selecting different combinations of factors such as the type of sweetener (e.g., sugar alcohols, stevia, or aspartame), the preservative used (e.g., natural or synthetic), the level of carbon dioxide for carbonation (e.g., low, medium, or high), and the acidity level (e.g., mild, moderate, or strong).

The following scenario will help us further understand how the multiplication of choices works:

Case scenario

A company is launching a new product in the market. To make sure that the marketing of the product is successful, the marketing team must determine the total number of advertisement variations based on these factors:

1. **Ad copy:** The company has 3 different slogans they can use.

2. **Visuals:** The product has 4 images that could be used for advertisement.

3. **Team:** Two groups are available, and either can lead the campaign.

4. **Platform:** The advertisement can be done on social media platforms, Facebook, X, or Instagram.

Find the total number of possible variations available to the marketing team.

Solution:

Using the multiplication of choices counting rule, we have:

1. Number of choices for ad copy ($n1$): $n1 = 3$ (three slogans available).

2. Number of choices for visuals ($n2$): $n2 = 4$ (four images available).

3. Number of choices for groups ($n3$): $n3 = 2$ (two groups that can lead the campaign).

4. Number of choices for platform ($n4$): $n4 = 3$ (three platforms available).

Now, using the multiplication of choices counting rule, we can find the total number of advertisement variations by multiplying the number of choices for each element:

Total variations $= n1 \times n2 \times n3 \times n4$

Total variations $= 3 \times 4 \times 2 \times 3$

Total variations $= 72$

The marketing team can create 72 different advertisements based on the factors.

2. Combination rule

Combinations refer to the arrangement or calculation of outcomes of an event in no specific order. Combinations are particularly useful in business for scenarios where the order of selection does not matter. One example is a hiring manager using the combination rule to calculate the number of ways to select a team of three employees from a group of ten candidates. In this case, the order in which they are chosen does not matter. Another example is marketers determining the number of ways to select a subset of products for a promotional bundle.

This rule helps businesses evaluate options efficiently, ensuring they can make smart decisions in resource allocation, project planning, and strategic selection.

The formula for calculating combinations is:

$$nCr = \frac{n!}{(n-r)!r!}$$

Read as the number of r selections or arrangements, or combinations from n objects or items.

Note: The combination can also be computed in Excel using: = COMBIN(n, r)

Case scenario A

5 members are to be selected from a pool of 10 qualified professionals. However, the order in which the employees are selected for the team does not matter. This scenario represents a combination problem because we are selecting a group of employees without considering the order of selection.

Scenario details:

- Total number of qualified employees available: $n = 10$
- Number of employees to be selected for the project team: $r = 5$

Using Combination Formula:

The number of combinations of (n) qualified employees taken (r) at a time is given by the combination formula:

$$nCr = \frac{n!}{(n-r)!r!}$$

Substituting the given values into the above formula, we get:

$$10C5 = \frac{10!}{(10-5)!5!} = \frac{10!}{5!5!}$$

$$10C5 = \frac{10!}{5!5!} = \frac{3628800}{120^*120}$$

$$10C5 = 252$$

Therefore, the company can form a total of 252 different project teams by selecting 5 employees from the pool of 10 qualified employees, without considering the order of selection. This understanding enables the company to assemble diverse teams with different skill sets and expertise. Thus, they can drive the new product development initiative forward effectively.

Case scenario B

A company needs to select 3 products for a promotional campaign. They have a total of 8 products to choose from. However, the order in which the products are selected for the campaign does not matter.

Scenario details:

- Total number of new available products: $n = 8$
- Number of products to be selected for the promotional campaign: $r = 3$

Combination Formula:

The number of combinations of (n) new products selected (r) at a time is given by the combination formula:

$$nCr = \frac{n!}{(n-r)!r!}$$

Substituting the given values into the formula:

$$8C3 = \frac{8!}{(8-3)!3!} = \frac{8!}{5!3!}$$

$$8C3 = \frac{8!}{5!3!} = \frac{40320}{120^*6}$$

$$8C3 = 56$$

The company has 56 different combinations to choose from.

3. Permutation rule

We have seen that the combination rule does not take into account the order when selecting objects. However, when using the permutation rule, the order of arrangement of the selected items or objects is a must, for instance, when arranging seating for VIP guests at an event. This ensures that specific individuals are placed in preferred positions.

In business, the concept of permutations is used to schedule tasks, arrange product displays, and analyze different order sequences to maximize efficiency. In marketing, permutations assist in testing different advertising strategies or pricing models to identify the most effective approach.

The formula for permutation is given by:

$$nPr = \frac{n!}{(n-r)!} = n(n-1)(n-2)\cdots(n-r+1)$$

Excel Computation: = PERMUT(n, r)

Where r is the number of objects to be selected, while n is the total number of objects.

Case scenario A

6 participants for a 6-seat roundtable discussion need to be seated for a business conference that a company is hosting. The order of seating is important to the firm because it wants to guarantee that every guest has a designated seat.

Solution:

Since the order of seating matters, this problem requires permutations.

Given:

- Total number of attendees: $n = 6$
- Number of seats: $r = 6$

Using the permutation formula:

$$nPr = \frac{n!}{(n-r)!}$$

$$6P6 = \frac{6!}{(6-6)!}$$

$$6P6 = 720$$

There are 720 different permutations for seating the 6 attendees at the roundtable discussion.

Case scenario B

Raw materials used by a manufacturing business include a broad variety of products, and, therefore, a company must select suppliers for them. It is required to rank 5 potential suppliers identified by the purchasing manager of the organization based on given factors such as cost, reliability, quality, and delivery time.

a. In how many ways can the 5 suppliers be arranged?

b. In how many ways can the top 3 suppliers be ordered?

Solution:

Given: Number of potential suppliers: $n = 5$

Part (A): Ranking all 5 suppliers:

Using permutations, we need to calculate the number of ways the purchasing manager can rank the 5 potential suppliers.

Using the permutation formula:

$$nPr = \frac{n!}{(n-r)!}$$

$$5P5 = \frac{5!}{(5-5)!}$$

$$5P5 = 120$$

There are 120 different ways the purchasing manager can rank all 5 potential suppliers.

Part (B): Ranking the top 3 suppliers:

Now, let's calculate the number of ways the purchasing manager can rank only the top 3 suppliers.

Using the permutation formula:

$$nPr = \frac{n!}{(n-r)!}$$

$$5P3 = \frac{5!}{(5-3)!}$$

$$5P3 = 60$$

There are 60 different ways the purchasing manager can rank the top 3 potential suppliers.

4. Multiplication of combinations

The "multiplication of combinations" is a technique used in combinatorics to calculate the total number of combinations or selections when choosing elements from multiple sets or groups. This method is used when selections are made from different sets with no specific requirement as to how the selections are made.

In business, this rule can be applied in the design of products, for instance, when choosing colors, sizes, and styles. In marketing, it can be used in selecting ad platforms and the target audience. In operations, it is useful in assembling supply chain routes to ensure efficient decision-making by considering all possible combinations.

This rule means that the summation of combinations or probabilities resulting from independent selections across multiple sets is obtained by multiplying the individual combinations or probabilities.

Total Combinations = Combinations from Set 1 × Combinations from Set 2 ×...× Combinations from Set n

Case scenario A

An organization needs to assemble a workforce in the form of a project team. In terms of the selection of the team, there are 6 developers and 4 designers to select from. The project manager has to select 3 developers and 2 designers to make a team of 5. How many possibilities can be generated?

Solution:

Given:

- Number of available developers: 6
- Number of available designers: 4
- Number of developers to be chosen: 3
- Number of designers to be chosen: 2

Using the multiplication of combinations method:

Total combinations = 6C3*4C2

$$6C3*4C2 = \frac{6!}{(6-3)!3!} * \frac{4!}{(4-2)!2!}$$

$$6C3*4C2 = \frac{720}{6*6} * \frac{24}{2*2} = 120$$

So, there are a total of 120 different possibilities for forming the project team.

Case scenario B

A company wants to form a budget allocation committee, consisting of 3 members from the finance department and 2 members from the technology department, to streamline its budgeting process. How many possible selections can the company make if it has to choose from 6 applicants in the technology department and 8 applicants in the finance department?

Solution:

Given:

- Number of finance department candidates: 8
- Number of technology department candidates: 6
- Number of finance department members to be chosen: 3
- Number of technology department members to be chosen: 2

Using the multiplication of combinations method:

Total Combinations = 8C3*6C2

$$8C3*6C2 = \frac{8!}{(8-3)!3!} * \frac{6!}{(6-2)!2!}$$

$$8C3*6C2 = \frac{40320}{120^*6} * \frac{720}{24^*2} = 840$$

So, there are a total of 840 different possibilities for selecting board members.

Case scenario 3

An e-commerce platform is creating product bundles to offer to customers. There are 5 electronic products and 4 accessory products available for bundling. The marketing team needs to select a bundle consisting of 3 electronic products and 2 accessory products. How many different possibilities are there?

Solution:
Given:

- Number of available electronic products: 5
- Number of available accessory products: 4
- Number of electronic products to be chosen: 3
- Number of accessory products to be chosen: 2

Using the multiplication of combinations method:

Total Combinations = 5C3*4C2

$$5C3*4C2 = \frac{5!}{(5-3)!3!} * \frac{4!}{(4-2)!2!}$$

$$5C3*4C2 = \frac{120}{2^*6} * \frac{24}{2^*2} = 60$$

So, there are a total of 60 different possibilities for creating product bundles.

5.2 Combining Probability and Counting Rules

Combining counting rules with probability rules offers a powerful framework for solving various types of probability problems. Specifically, when dealing with problems involving conditional probability of combinations, a systematic approach leveraging both counting and probability principles is essential.

In these kinds of situations, the probability of each particular event happening is represented by multiplying all of the sub-combinations together. The entire number of possible outcomes is then divided by the overall combination.

Imagine a situation in which an organization is choosing a project team from a group of workers with various skill levels. The project manager needs to determine the probability of choosing a team with particular roles based on predetermined standards.

Let's break down the process:

1. **Identify sub-combinations**

    Define the sub-combinations representing the probabilities of selecting individuals for each role within the team. For instance, the team may need a chairperson, secretary, and vice chairperson, and therefore, we have to determine the probability of filling each position separately.

2. **Apply counting rules**

    To get the total number of potential combinations for each sub-combination, we apply counting procedures, such as permutations or combinations. In this step, we determine the number of ways each role can be filled in relation to the pool of available employees.

3. **Calculate conditional probabilities**

    Multiply the probabilities of each sub-combination together. This step represents the joint probability of selecting individuals for all required roles, simultaneously. To get the conditional probability of a specific combination, the conditional probability is first sought and divided by the total number of possible combinations.

4. Interpret results

Interpret the probability obtained. The calculated conditional probability provides insights into the likelihood of selecting the desired combination of roles for the project team, based on available employees.

Case scenario A

A store has 9 lifestyle magazines and 7 real estate magazines on the counter. If two customers purchased a magazine, find the probability that one of the magazines was purchased.

Solution:

Given:

- Number of lifestyle magazines: 9
- Number of real estate magazines: 7
- Total number of magazines: 16

The total number of combinations is 16C2, and the sub-combinations are 9C1 and 7C1. Then the solution to this problem is:

$$\frac{9C1*7C1}{16C2} = \frac{9^*7}{120} = 0.525$$

When the order is important, the number of desired selections is divided by the total number of permutations.

Case scenario B

A company is conducting a training session for its employees. 4 men and 4 women are participating in the training. Groups of 3 need to be formed in order to participate in team-building activities. What is the probability of forming a group with at least 1 woman included?

Solution:

Calculate the total number of permutations:

Since the order of selection matters (permutations), we'll calculate the total number of possible permutations of participants in groups of 3.

Total permutations = 8P3

$$nPr = \frac{n!}{(n-r)!}$$

$$8P3 = \frac{8!}{(8-3)!} = 336$$

Next, we'll calculate the number of permutations where at least one woman is included in the group:

a) One woman and two men:

Number of permutations = 4P1 × 4P2

$$4P1 \times 4P2 = \frac{4!}{(4-1)!} \times \frac{4!}{(4-2)!}$$

$$4P1 \times 4P2 = 4 \times 12 = 48$$

b) Two women and one man:

$$4P1 \times 4P2 = \frac{4!}{(4-2)!} \times \frac{4!}{(4-1)!}$$

$$4P1 \times 4P2 = 12 \times 4 = 48$$

c) Three women:

Number of permutations = 4P3

$$4P3 = \frac{4!}{(4-3)!} = 24$$

Total permutations with at least one woman:
48 + 48 + 24 = 120

Calculate the probability:

The probability of forming a group with at least one woman =

$$\frac{Number\ of\ permutations\ with\ at\ least\ one\ woman}{Total\ permutations}$$

$$= \frac{120}{336} = 0.35714$$

The probability of getting a group where at least one woman exists, among the people chosen, is 0.35714. This implies a 35.714% chance that a group will be formed having at least one woman in it.

Concluding this section marks the end of Chapter Five. In this chapter, we have explored the fundamental principles of counting rules and their integration with probability. This gives us access to powerful tools for analyzing complex scenarios and solving probabilistic problems. By mastering these concepts, we can now calculate probabilities in diverse situations with accuracy and confidence.

In the next chapter, we will shift our focus to the methods of selecting representative samples from populations, enabling reliable data analysis for effective decision-making.

Chapter Summary

- Factorial notation ($k!$) allows systematic enumeration and combination of all possible scenarios or outcomes. They play a crucial role in analyzing permutations and combinations in business contexts.

- The multiplication of choices rule calculates the total number of outcomes in multi-stage events by multiplying the choices at each stage.

- Combinations refer to the arrangement of outcomes where the order doesn't matter.

- The combination formula given by $nCr = \dfrac{n!}{(n-r)!r!}$ is used to calculate the number of ways of selecting some objects from a set of objects when the order is not needed.

- Permutations involve the arrangement of selected items or objects where the order matters.

- The permutation formula is given by $nPr = \dfrac{n!}{(n-r)!}$. Permutation is used when the order of selecting some objects from a set of objects is important.

- The multiplication of combinations rule is useful for calculating the total number of combinations or selections when choosing elements from multiple sets or groups.

- Probability and counting rules can be combined to solve various types of probability problems, particularly those involving conditional probability of combinations.

- By systematically applying both counting and probability principles, organizations can analyze complex scenarios, optimize resource allocation, and make informed decisions.

Further Learning

(Links also available in Online Resources)

1. **Permutations and combinations**
   http://bit.ly/4mSf94h

2. **Probability using permutations and combinations**
   http://bit.ly/3HltORI

Quiz

1. **What is a factorial?**
   a. A type of marketing strategy
   b. The product of all positive integers up to a given number
   c. A type of subscription plan

2. **A company needs to select 3 marketing strategies from the 5 options available. In how many different ways can they select the 3 marketing strategies? (Hint: Combination rule)**
   a. 8
   b. 10
   c. 15

3. **In how many ways can 10 business people be seated in a row if 3 of them must sit together? In how many ways can 3 out of 10 business people be seated in 3 available chairs, if the order in which they sit matters? (Hint: Use permutation rules.)**
   a. 720
   b. 600
   c. 120

4. **A software company offers 4 subscription plans, each with 3 different features. How many different subscription packages can a customer choose from? (Hint: Multiplication rule)**
   a. 7
   b. 10
   c. 12

5. A restaurant offers 5 beers, 6 wines, and 4 energy drinks. How many different beverage combinations could a customer select? (Hint: Multiplication rule)

   a. 10
   b. 120
   c. 30

6. Define the combination rule:

   a. The arrangement of objects in a specific order
   b. The multiplication of choices counting rule
   c. The selection of objects without considering the order

7. Which Excel formula can be used to compute a combination problem?

   a. = PERMUT (n,r)
   b. = COMBIN (n,r)
   c. = FACT (n, a)

8. Define the permutation rule:

   a. The arrangement of objects in a specific order
   b. The selection of objects without considering the order
   c. The product of all positive integers up to a given number

9. Give the Excel formula that can be used to solve a permutation problem:

   a. = PERMUT (n,r)
   b. = COMBIN (n,r)
   c. = MULT (n,a)

10. A team of 4 engineers needs to be selected from ten candidates. How many different teams can be selected? (Hint: Combination rule)

   a. 120
   b. 210
   c. 252

CHAPTER 6

Sampling and Sampling Techniques

Key Learning Objectives

- Define terminologies in sampling.
- Understand planning for a sample survey.
- Learn the importance of sampling.
- Gain insight into sampling bias and sampling errors.
- Explore sampling techniques.

Armed with an in-depth understanding of the various methods used to collect data, which we gained early on in Chapter Two, we are now at the right inflection point to learn the process of sampling, selection of samples, and various sampling techniques in this chapter.

The selection of samples from populations is central to data collection and statistical analyses. Sampling allows researchers to save precious time and resources that would have been utilized if the entire population were studied. It provides the necessary framework for designing studies and interpreting results.

The process of sampling is not easy; the researcher needs to ensure that the selected sample is representative of the general population. They also need to ensure that the results from the statistical analysis of the sample are reliable.

Understanding the behavior of sample statistics is crucial as it informs about sampling distributions. Sampling distributions illustrate how sample statistics are distributed if multiple samples are taken from a population. They also enable inferences to be made about the population and help in estimating uncertainty.

6.1 Terminologies in Sampling

To understand sampling and sampling techniques effectively, it is essential to familiarize oneself with the most common terminologies. This section introduces the foundational terms and concepts used in sampling. We have covered some of these terms in Chapter One, Section 1.4, but we will study them here again as they are specifically relevant to sampling.

1. **Population**

   The population is the entire group or set of individuals or elements that the researcher is interested in studying. The population for a study on employee satisfaction might include all the employees working at a particular company.

2. **Census**

   This refers to the complete enumeration of the population.

3. **Sample survey**

   A sample survey is an enumeration that involves collecting data from a portion or subset of the population. Sample surveys are usually cheaper compared to complete enumeration (census).

4. **Sample**

A sample is a subset of the population selected for study or analysis. A company might conduct a sample survey of its customers to gather feedback on product satisfaction.

5. **Sampling**

It is the procedure of choosing a sample of the population to be used in the study. The main goal of sampling is to come up with a sample that in one way or the other represents the population.

6. **Observational unit**

It refers to the entity or individual on which observations are made or data is collected. In a retail business, the observational unit could be individual customers purchasing products.

7. **Sampling unit**

A sampling unit refers to the entity or individual selected from the population during the sampling process. In market research, the sampling unit might be the households selected to participate in a survey about consumer preferences.

8. **Sampling frame**

This refers to the list or source from which the sample is drawn.

9. **Sampling techniques**

These are the different ways researchers use when selecting items or units from the target population to form the sample.

10. Statistical induction

It is a process that generalizes the conclusions derived from the statistical analyses of samples to the entire population.

11. Sampling interval

It is the distance between observations selected from the population to be included in the sample.

6.2 Considerations for Planning a Sample Survey

A survey is an important technique in sampling because it allows researchers to collect data efficiently from a representative sample of a larger population. Sample surveys provide insights into characteristics, behaviors, or opinions while minimizing costs and time compared to conducting a population census. Various factors need to be put into careful consideration to ensure that the survey results are reliable and useful for decision-making. They include:

1. Objectives of the survey

- The general objectives of the survey should be identified and, from them, specific objectives can be clearly outlined.
- Specifying the objectives ensures that the researcher remains focused on the study.

2. Population to be sampled

- The target population for the study should be identified.
- List and define all the attributes and characteristics of the target population.

3. Data to be collected

- Specify the key variables or measures that will be collected to address the research objectives.
- Design a structured questionnaire or data collection instrument to gather relevant information.
- Every data item to be collected should be relevant to the objectives of the study.

4. Selection of the sample

- Every sampling method has its challenges and advantages; each sampling method is suitable for a different type of population.
- It is crucial to select a sampling method that will help pick the most representative sample of the population.

5. Degree of accuracy

- Specify the degree of accuracy of the results.
- Ensure that the sample is not too small such that it impacts the degree of accuracy.
- Use advanced instruments and tools to reduce any errors in measurements.

6. Methods of measurement

- Ensure that each variable is measured using the correct scale: either nominal, ordinal, or ratio scale.
- The instruments should have high validity and reliability to minimize chances of error.

7. Pre-test

- This stage allows the researcher to test the various tools or instruments to be used in the study.

- The questionnaires may be evaluated with respect to the clarity of their questions.

- A pre-test may help in estimating the cost of the study and also reveal challenges that the researcher may encounter in the study.

8. Organization of the field work

- Organize the training of field enumerators.

- Think of potential strategies and solutions that could be used to address possible problems in the course of the study.

9. Summary and analysis

- Clean the data and determine how the missing responses will be treated.

- Determine which method is appropriate for conducting analysis on the data.

6.3 Reasons for Sampling

Sampling is often preferred over conducting a census due to several practical reasons related to time, finance, and logistics:

1. Time efficiency

- Enumerating the whole population requires a lot of time. Carrying out sampling cuts down the time, given that only a proportion of the population is selected for analysis.

- Carrying out a sample survey ensures that results are achieved more quickly.

2. Financial considerations

- Carrying out a census requires more finances to facilitate wider coverage. The cost is even more if the population being studied is sparsely distributed.
- Sample surveys cut down the costs. Sampling ensures that researchers maximize their budgets while still obtaining meaningful insights.

3. Logistical challenges

- Sampling makes data collection manageable and improves response rates.
- Planning a census requires complex logistical organization. The researcher needs to plan the transportation to the field, security of the field staff, accommodation, and many other details. These factors make a census a much more strenuous process than a sample survey.

6.4 Sampling Bias

Sampling bias refers to errors and inaccuracies caused by selecting a sample that is not representative of the population. Sampling biases have the potential to influence the validity and generalizability of findings.

The following are some sources of sampling biases:

1. Incorrect identification of the target population may lead to the exclusion of the correct population units and the inclusion of units not relevant to the study.

2. Including convenient units or items of the population when the correct units are unavailable for sampling.

3. Using a sampling frame that does not fit the population.

4. Including volunteers in the sample or individuals who self-select.

5. Using an outdated sampling frame.

6. The researcher is opting to select every n-th item or unit when there is a pattern or periodicity in the population. This may lead to a selection bias, especially if the sampling interval aligns with a natural cycle or repeating trend within the population. This leads to overrepresentation or underrepresentation of certain characteristics.

7. Using clustering methods and selecting some clusters for analysis when the clusters are not representative of the population.

8. Failure of the respondents in the sample to show up during the actual enumeration.

6.5 Types of Errors in Sampling

We have seen that sample surveys involve studying only a subset or portion of the population and as such some amount of inaccuracy from the information collected naturally arises. Therefore, sampling errors occur on the account of sampling and generally happen to be random variations in the sample estimates around the true population parameters. These errors include:

1. Sampling error

A sampling error is the natural difference between the outcomes of a sample and the results that would have been derived from the entire population (Sampling error = Statistic from sample – True population parameter).

2. Margin of error

A margin of error is the critical value at a specified confidence level multiplied by the standard error of the sample statistic.

3. Frame error

A frame error is brought about by differences in the target population and the sampling frame used for the sample. The researcher might include some items or units not part of the target population or exclude items or units which are part of the target population in the sampling frame used to select the sample.

4. Chance error

This error arises by virtue of the natural variability and randomness that occurs when a sample is selected and used for analysis instead of the entire population. The estimates obtained from the analysis could deviate from the true population analysis, thereby giving rise to chance error.

5. Response error

A response error arises when the respondents provide inaccurate and incomplete answers during the survey.

6.6 Sampling Techniques

Sampling techniques are the methods with which the researchers are able to choose the sample from the population of interest. Each method comes with its strengths and weaknesses. The difference between these techniques is in how they are implemented. Let's understand these techniques in detail:

Figure 6.1 Sampling techniques

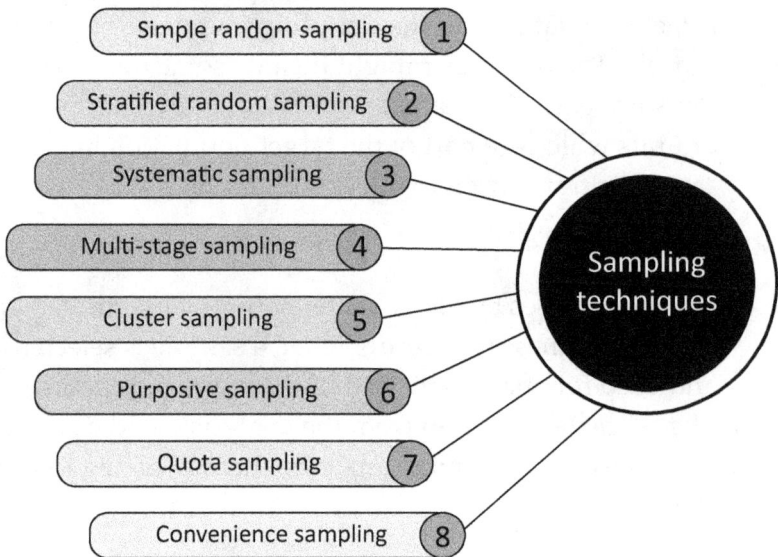

6.6.1 Simple Random Sampling

In statistical research, one of the most fundamental and popular sampling techniques is Simple Random Sampling (SRS). SRS is characterized by its simplicity and fairness in choosing units or items from a population to include in a sample.

Simple random sampling occurs when each unit or item in the population of interest has an equal and independent chance of being selected, and none of the selections is affected by any other. Thus, the probability of each element of the population, which is of size N, being included in the sample is equal to $\dfrac{1}{N}$.

If we want to ensure that every single unit of the population is included in the sample once, the units are always drawn from the population one at a time without replacement.

Suppose a sample size of n is to be drawn from a population of size N, then the sample can be obtained in NCn. This is a combination problem expressed as:

$$NCn = \frac{N!}{(N-n)!n!}$$

The probability of selecting a unit from the population only once can be given as:

$$\frac{1}{NCn} = \frac{(N-n)!n!}{N!}$$

Once the first unit has been selected, the other remaining units have the same probability of being included in the sample in a simple random sampling without replacement.

Process of simple random sampling:

The following steps outline the process of simple random sampling:

1. Specify the target population and verify that every unit or item has a unique identification. This ensures that each individual unit is part of the simple random sampling process.

2. Units are randomly selected using various randomization techniques. Randomization techniques include random number generators and the use of computers.

3. The researcher determines the sample size. The preferred sample size should be manageable for the researcher i.e., it should not be too large or too small.

4. Once a researcher has determined the preferred size of the sample, units that meet the inclusion criteria are selected to form the sample.

Consider a supermarket that wants to evaluate the effectiveness of its customer service. They decide to carry out a survey to gather feedback from customers who shopped with them in the last week. Records at the supermarket show that 6,000 customers shopped in the past week with their information stored.

The attendants use a random number generator to select 500 shopping receipts from all 6000 customers randomly. The phone numbers of the selected customers are retrieved from their receipts; these are used to contact the customers and get their feedback.

By randomly selecting customers, each customer has an equal chance of being selected. The supermarket can then analyze the survey results to evaluate the effectiveness of their customer service and make data-driven adjustments for future campaigns.

Sample estimates in simple random sampling:

Sample mean:

Sample mean $\bar{x} = \dfrac{1}{n}\sum\limits_{i=1}^{n} xi$

Population mean:

$$\bar{x} = \dfrac{1}{N}\sum\limits_{i=1}^{N} xi$$

Sample variance:

$$s^2 = \frac{1}{n-1}\sum(xi-\bar{x})^2 = \frac{1}{n-1}\left(\sum xi^2 - n\bar{x}^2\right)$$

Population variance:

$$S^2 = \frac{1}{N-1}\sum(xi-\bar{X})^2 = \frac{1}{N-1}\left(\sum xi^2 - N\bar{X}^2\right)$$

Considering that α is the significance level (0.05 for 95 confidence level) and $t_{\alpha/2}$ is the critical value from the t-distribution corresponding to a two-tailed test at the chosen α level (see Chapter Seven for more details), the confidence limits for the population mean $\bar{X}$ are:

$$\bar{X} = \bar{x} \pm z_{\alpha/2}\sqrt{\left(\frac{N-n}{N}\right)\frac{s^2}{n}} \quad \text{for sample size n} > 30$$

$$\bar{X} = \bar{x} \pm t_{\alpha/2,}n-1\sqrt{\left(\frac{N-n}{N}\right)\frac{s^2}{n}} \quad \text{for sample size n} \leq 30$$

The confidence interval for the population mean $\bar{X}$:

$$\bar{x} - z_{\alpha/2}\sqrt{\left(\frac{N-n}{N}\right)\frac{s^2}{n}} \leq_X \leq \bar{x} + z_{\alpha/2}\sqrt{\left(\frac{N-n}{N}\right)\frac{s^2}{n}} \quad \text{for sample}$$

size n > 30

$$\bar{x} - t_{\alpha/2,}n-1\sqrt{\left(\frac{N-n}{N}\right)\frac{s^2}{n}} \leq_x \leq \bar{x} + t_{\alpha/2,n}n-1\sqrt{\left(\frac{N-n}{N}\right)\frac{s^2}{n}} \quad \text{for}$$

sample size n ≤ 30

Confidence limits for the population total X:

$$X = N\bar{x} \pm z_{\alpha/2}\sqrt{N(N-n)\frac{s^2}{n}} \quad \text{for sample size n} > 30$$

$$X = N\bar{x} \pm t_{\alpha/2,}n-1\sqrt{N(N-n)\frac{s^2}{n}} \quad \text{for sample size n} \leq 30$$

Advantages of Simple Random Sampling (SRS)

- Every individual item has an equal probability of making the sample. This ensures that the sample selected is representative of the population.
- SRS forms a foundation upon which other sophisticated sampling techniques are based.
- It is easy to use.

Limitations of SRS:

- A lot of time is needed if the population is large.
- A smaller sample size may not be representative of the population.
- It is difficult to compile the sampling frame if the population is large.
- Assigning identification numbers to large populations could be difficult.
- It is not suitable where a population is heterogeneous.

6.6.2 Stratified Random Sampling

The stratified sampling technique focuses on partitioning the entire target population into portions known as strata. Each stratum has units or items which have the same characteristics. Simple random sampling is used within each stratum to select a sub-sample. All the sub-samples are combined into the final sample for analysis. Stratified random sampling is suitable when the target population is heterogeneous.

Process of stratified random sampling:

The following steps outline the process of stratified random sampling:

1. Divide the target population into strata. Each stratum must contain only individual items which are homogenous i.e., have the same characteristics.

2. Determine the required sample size. Randomly select sub-samples from the strata based on the sub-population of each stratum relative to the entire population. The researcher is at will to determine how many items to select from each stratum as long as it helps in addressing the objectives.

3. Combine the sub-samples from the strata to form a final sample.

Consider a bank that wants to understand customer satisfaction levels across different income groups to improve its services. Since varied income levels can significantly influence customer satisfaction, the bank uses stratified random sampling.

Stratification steps: The bank categorizes customers into three income groups: low-income, middle-income, and high-income, and samples 30 customers from each income group to ensure balanced representation. Finally, they combine the participants and carry out the survey.

Advantages of stratified random sampling:

- When used for heterogeneous populations, it eliminates bias, thereby increasing precision.
- Heterogeneous populations produce diversified samples, thereby providing better representation of the population.

- Researchers have better control over the subgroups as they can vary the selection of items in each strata for better representation of the population.

Limitations of stratified random sampling:

- There could be instances of overlap if items or units fall in more than one stratum.
- It is time consuming given that the sampling frame for the whole population must be compiled.

6.6.3 Systematic Sampling

This method requires the researcher to pick a random start and then pick every n-th element or item from the population. This sampling technique is the most preferred one for large and homogenous populations.

Process of systematic sampling:

The following steps outline the process of systematic sampling:

1. Specify the target population.
2. Determine the desired sample size.
3. Determine the sampling interval, k, by dividing the population size (N) with the sample size (n) as shown below:

$$\text{Sampling interval: } k = \frac{N}{n}$$

4. Choose a random start that is between the first element and the sampling interval, k. The selection ensures that there is fairness for each element to appear in the sample. Once a random start has been decided, every k-th element is selected until the sample size is reached.

Consider a hotel that wants to get feedback on the meals they serve. They decide to use systematic sampling for efficiency. The hotel estimates that 400 customers are served daily. They decide to survey every 10th customer who walks through the door.

To ensure randomness in the starting point, they use a random number generator to pick a number between 1 and 10. Suppose the generator picks 5, the survey begins with the 5th customer and continues with every 10th customer thereafter (15th, 25th, 35th, and so on).

This systematic approach ensures the sample is evenly spread throughout the day, providing diverse customer opinions while saving time compared to a fully random process.

Advantages of systematic sampling:

- A random start eliminates bias.
- The method ensures that the target population is covered comprehensively.
- Simple and easy to use.

Limitations of systematic sampling:

- Populations that have patterns or periodicity may introduce bias in the selection of the sample.
- Systematic sampling may not be suitable for populations with irregular patterns or structures. It is wise to consider other sampling techniques such as stratified or cluster sampling where systematic sampling is not applicable.

6.6.4 Multi-Stage Sampling

Multi-stage sampling involves classifying a population into hierarchical blocks and selecting a sample in each block. The method is suitable for large heterogeneous populations.

Process of multi-stage sampling:

The following steps outline the process of multi-stage sampling:

1. **Dividing the population into hierarchical blocks (stages)**

   - Start with dividing the population into hierarchical blocks. These blocks could be a hierarchy of geographical boundaries, administration or any other attributes.

   - The clusters should ideally be heterogeneous within themselves but homogenous between them.

2. **Selection of stages**

   - Simple random sampling is used to select blocks/ stages from the population. The number of blocks is at the discretion of the researcher, time and resources.

3. **Selection of samples within clusters**

   - Upon selection of blocks, other sampling methods are used to select elements from each block.

   - The sampling method to be used in each block for the selection of the elements should ensure that every element has an equal chance of appearing in the sample.

4. Optional additional stages

- In some cases, multi-stage sampling may involve additional stages of sampling. For example, if the selected clusters themselves contain subgroups that need to be sampled separately, additional stages may be added to the sampling process.

Consider a multinational company that wants to assess employee satisfaction across its global offices. Conducting surveys for all employees worldwide is impractical, so the company uses multi-stage sampling.

Here's how they implement it:

1. **First stage:** They divide their offices into clusters based on continents, e.g., North America, Europe, Asia.
2. **Second stage:** Within each selected continent, they randomly select a few countries, e.g., the USA, Germany, and India.
3. **Third stage:** Within the selected countries, they randomly choose specific office locations, e.g., New York, Berlin, and Bangalore.
4. **Fourth stage:** Within the selected office locations, they randomly sample a subset of employees to participate in the survey.

This approach allows the company to manage costs and logistics while ensuring representation from multiple levels of the organization.

Advantages of multi-stage sampling:

- It is particularly suitable for populations that are difficult to access or enumerate comprehensively. By using existing administrative boundaries or other natural groupings as clusters, researchers can simplify the sampling process.

- Multi-stage sampling brings flexibility by allowing researchers to use suitable sampling methods in each block while selecting elements.

Limitations of multi-stage sampling:

- Randomly selecting blocks gives room for potential bias as the selected blocks may not be representative of the population.
- Multi-stage sampling is a complex method requiring caution when selecting the blocks and when selecting elements from each block.

6.6.5 Cluster Sampling

This method is based on the assumption that a population is composed of distinct identifiable units on which sampling can be done. It is sometimes used when researchers are not able to directly sample individuals in the population but can sample groups (clusters) instead. The population is divided into clusters from which a sample of clusters is selected.

Process of cluster sampling:

The following steps outline the process of cluster sampling:

1. **Dividing the population into clusters**

   - These clusters are based on identifiable units within the population.
   - The clusters should ideally be heterogeneous within themselves but homogenous between them.

2. Selecting clusters randomly

- Use simple random sampling to select the clusters randomly.
- The number of clusters depends on the researcher, resources and relevancy to the objectives.

3. Sampling within selected clusters

- A random sampling of elements is done on the clusters to select elements that are combined to make the final sample.

Consider a national retail chain that wants to evaluate customer satisfaction across its stores but conducting surveys at every location is impractical due to time and cost constraints. The company decides to use cluster sampling.

They group their stores into clusters based on geographical regions such as Northeast, Midwest, South, and West, from which they randomly select a few regions, e.g., Midwest and South. Within the selected regions, they survey all customers who visited specific stores during a given time frame.

By sampling clusters instead of the entire population, the company reduces costs while still obtaining valuable insights that are likely representative of customer satisfaction across the regions.

Advantages of cluster sampling:

- This method is suitable when the population is large and dispersed. Dealing with clusters minimizes costs and other logistical demands.
- Dividing the target population into clusters allows the researcher to manage the population effectively.

Limitations of cluster sampling:

- It is impossible to eliminate bias when clusters are not representative of the target population.
- Clusters may share sampling units or elements, thereby bringing intra-cluster correlation, which could reduce the degree of accuracy of the results.

The three sampling techniques explained below are less commonly used than those discussed above; therefore, we'll cover them briefly.

6.6.6 Quota Sampling

Researchers employ quota sampling when they are focussing on a specific attribute that is present in the target population. Quota sampling does not involve random sampling as it is a non-probability sampling technique. The researcher instead chooses individuals based on pre-established quotas or criteria to guarantee that particular traits are represented in the sample.

Consider a coffee processing factory that wants to launch a new coffee product in the market and intends to survey users to get their feedback. They employ quota sampling to ensure they get feedback across ages and genders.

The company sets the following quotas for their sample:

- 40% of respondents should be women aged 18–35.
- 30% should be men aged 18–35.
- 20% should be women aged 36–50.
- 10% should be men aged 36–50.

Surveyors are instructed to stop interviewing participants once the quotas for each category are filled. This method ensures the sample reflects the intended proportions of the population while allowing for a non-random selection process within each quota.

6.6.7 Convenience Sampling

Convenience sampling is a non-probability sampling technique, whereby the researcher selects people or objects randomly in a given community taking into consideration their ease of access. Convenience sampling is not as rigorous as other probability sampling methods since the participation of the members is not randomly chosen but based on ease of availability.

Consider an apparel store chain that wants to gather quick feedback on a new collection they plan to launch. To save time and resources, the management decides to collect opinions from customers who visit their busiest location during lunch hours over the next two days.

Instead of using a randomized method, the feedback is gathered from customers who are conveniently available at that location and time. While this method is fast and cost-effective, it may not represent the opinions of all customers across different locations, times, or demographics. Despite its limitations, the data collected can provide initial insights to guide further decisions.

6.6.8 Purposive Sampling

This technique of non-probability sampling is also known as purposive, intentional or judgmental sampling whereby the researcher deliberately chooses the items or participants from the population under study depending on certain important characteristics or interests. While in purposive (non-probability) sampling the selection process involves a conscious and intentional process of selecting the subject

samplings, probability samplings ensure that the selected sample represents the overall population.

Imagine a beverage manufacturer who wants to know the preferences of high-income customers for their newest premium beverage brand. The manufacturer prefers to intentionally select customers who earn $400,000 and get their opinion on their preferences.

By specifically targeting this demographic, the company ensures the feedback comes from individuals who are more likely to be potential buyers of their premium product. This approach allows the manufacturer to focus on insights that are directly relevant to their target market, making purposive sampling an effective strategy for this scope.

In this chapter, we have explored the essential aspects of sampling, including key terminologies, the process of planning a sample survey, and the importance of sampling in research. We also examined potential pitfalls such as sampling bias and errors, as well as various sampling techniques and their applications. Additionally, sampling techniques provide insights into how sample statistics relate to the population. With a strong foundation in sampling, we now transition to inferential statistics beginning with the study of correlation, where we will explore relationships between variables and their significance in uncovering patterns and trends!

Chapter Summary

- Sampling plays a crucial role in business analytics since it enables firms to obtain samples and gather valuable information regarding the population in question in the shortest time possible.

- Sampling is the process of choosing a small number of people, items or cases from a larger population and it takes into account factors such as sample size and sampling techniques that are used.

- The important steps in planning a sample survey include the development of objectives, identification of population, identification of variables to be measured, choice of sampling methods, defining the degree of accuracy, conducting pre-tests, preparation of field work activities, analysis, and conclusion over findings.

- The purpose of sampling is to save on cost and time.

- Sampling bias arises when the samples selected for a study are not in any way a true reflection of the population, and therefore, the results and conclusions drawn in the study are systematically biased.

- Sampling errors include chance errors: random fluctuations that occur in the whole sampling process, frame errors: inaccuracies in the sampling frame used in the whole sampling process, and response errors: inaccuracies in the answers given by the respondents.

- In simple random sampling, every unit or individual has the same probability of being included in the sample.

- Stratified random sampling divides the population into homogeneous strata, improving precision and representation.

- Systematic sampling selects every n-th element from a population list after a random start, offering simplicity and efficiency.

- Multi-stage sampling divides the population into clusters and selects samples at each stage, suitable for large, heterogeneous populations.

- Cluster sampling selects clusters from the population and samples all individuals within chosen clusters, being cost-effective for dispersed populations.

- Quota sampling is useful when a specific attribute in the target population is of interest to the researcher.

- Selection of units or individuals under convenience sampling is based on ease of accessibility to the researcher, while it is based on intention and judgment under purposive sampling.

Further Learning

(Links also available in Online Resources)

1. **Types of sampling**
   http://bit.ly/4lzJcN8

2. **Sampling distributions**
   http://bit.ly/45AiEp2

3. **Methods of sampling from a population**
   http://bit.ly/41FtoBi

Quiz

1. **What is the primary purpose of sampling in business statistics?**
   a. To collect data from the entire population
   b. To accurately estimate population parameters
   c. To ensure complete representation of the population

2. **There are two types of enumeration: census and survey. How do they differ?**
   a. A census refers to complete enumeration while a survey refers to enumeration of a sample.
   b. A survey is the complete enumeration of the population, while a census is the enumeration of a portion of the population.
   c. Census and survey both refer to the enumeration of the population.

3. **Sampling distributions describe:**
   a. The distribution of sample statistics obtained from multiple samples
   b. The distribution of population parameters
   c. The distribution of individual data points in a sample

4. **Which one of the following is a key consideration in planning a sample survey?**
   a. Determining the population parameters
   b. Identifying the target population
   c. Conducting a census of the population

5. **Sampling bias occurs when:**
   a. The sample accurately represents the population.
   b. The sample does not accurately represent the population.
   c. The sample size is too small.

6. **Which statement is true about simple random sampling?**
   a. Every unit or individual in the population has the same probability of being in the sample.
   b. It requires minimal resources and expertise.
   c. It divides the population into homogeneous strata.

7. **In stratified random sampling, strata are formed based on:**
   a. The researcher's intuition
   b. Characteristics that are relevant to the research objectives
   c. The alphabetical order of the population

8. **Systematic sampling involves:**
   a. Selecting every n-th element from a list after a random start
   b. Dividing the population into clusters and randomly selecting some of these clusters
   c. Selecting clusters from the population and sampling all individuals within chosen clusters

9. **Multi-stage sampling is particularly useful:**
   a. When the population is small and homogeneous
   b. For large heterogeneous populations
   c. When every element in the population has an equal chance of being selected

10. **Cluster sampling involves:**
    a. Selecting every n-th element from a list after a random start
    b. Dividing the population into strata and selecting samples at each stratum
    c. Dividing population into clusters, randomly selecting clusters, and sampling individuals within chosen clusters

Answers

1 – c	2 – a	3 – a	4 – b	5 – b
6 – a	7 – b	8 – a	9 – b	10 – c

CHAPTER 7

Correlation Analysis

Key Learning Objectives

- Learn how to measure the correlation between variables.
- Interpret the values of the correlation coefficient.
- Test the significance of the correlation coefficient.
- Understand the usage of a scatter plot to test the significance of the correlation coefficient.

Problem-solving in a business setup begins by identifying the relationship or association between the factors involved; in business statistics, these factors are better known as variables. For instance, we might want to know the relationship between demand and supply or that between direction and magnitude. This knowledge helps explain and optimize outcomes between the variables.

This chapter introduces you to the concept of association and relationship between variables known as correlation. Correlation is a statistical method that establishes the magnitude of associations as well as the direction of the relationship between variables. A correlation does not point out which variable is resulting in the other. However, for quantitative variables, it is possible to explain the strength and direction of the linear relation. It is important to note that the Pearson correlation, which calculates the linear relationship between two numerical variables, is the correlation under discussion in this chapter.

7.1. Measuring Correlation Between Variables

Every statistical software can be utilized in testing and determining the association between variables. In Excel, correlation can be obtained using the formula: CORREL (A2:A9, B2:B9), followed by pressing Enter, if it is known that the values of variable A are in cells A2 to A9 and that of variable B are in cells B2 to B9. The value obtained in the end through this calculation is referred to as the coefficient of correlation between variable A and variable B.

The correlation coefficient obtained is denoted as r and ρ for a sample and population, respectively.

Example

Determine the correlation coefficient between the number of customers that visited an electronics shop and the sales (in thousand dollars) made by the shop on each of the three days, given the information below.

Table 7.1   Sales made by the shop on each of the three days

Day 1		Day 2		Day 3	
Customers	Sales	Customers	Sales	Customers	Sales
80	100	20	30	44	28
90	80	40	44	86	87

Day 1		Day 2		Day 3	
Customers	Sales	Customers	Sales	Customers	Sales
100	56	77	76	56	55
121	51	38	54	55	100
70	140	98	99	88	32
82	110	102	110	45	89
100	93	78	80	33	33
55	167	20	19	59	62
44	180	30	35	38	30
60	170	88	88	12	15
80	135	84	98	15	60
20	220	65	67	67	66

The correlation coefficient can be obtained using the Excel function CORREL as shown below in Figure 7.1.

Figure 7.1 CORREL function in Excel

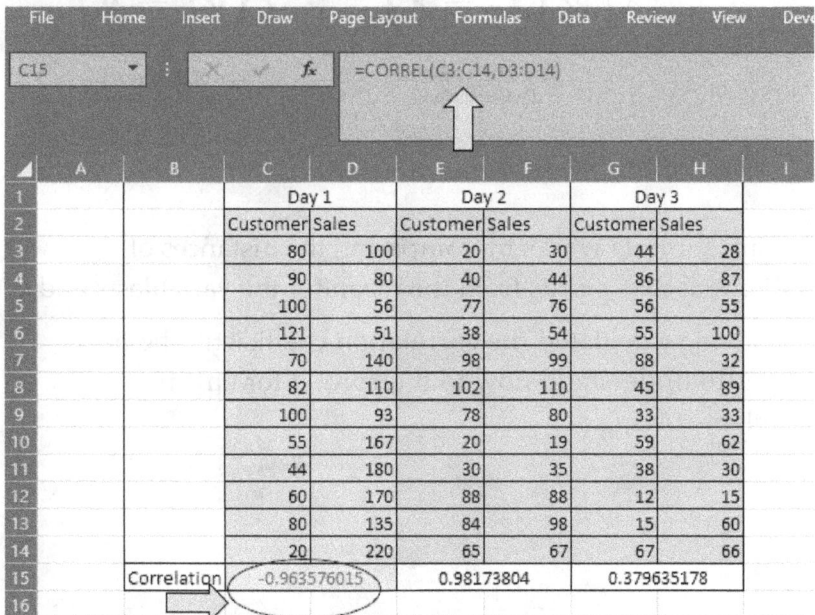

Calculating the coefficient of correlation:

The formula for computing the coefficient of correlation is given as:

$$r = \frac{\sum[(xi - \bar{x})(yi - \bar{y})]}{\sqrt{\sum(xi - \bar{x})^2 \sum(yi - \bar{y})^2}}$$

Where:

Figure 7.2 Formula for computing the coefficient of correlation

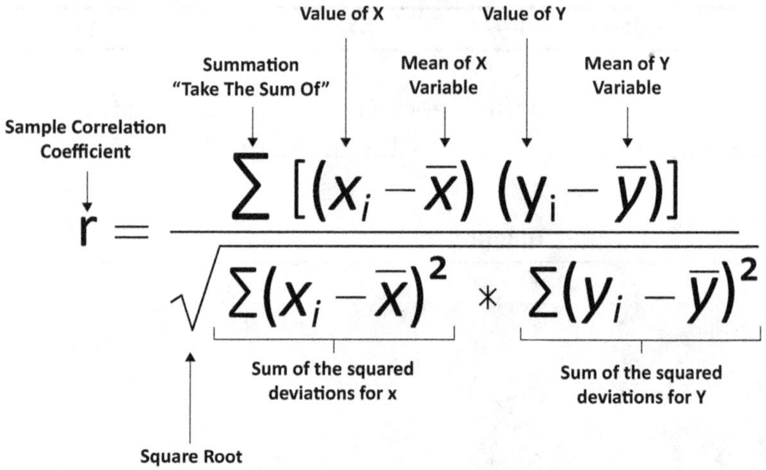

This formula works by comparing the distances of individual data points from the mean for the variables x and y.

Having calculated the correlation coefficient, the next step is to understand how to interpret it for effective problem-solving.

7.2 Interpreting the Values of the Coefficient of Correlation

The coefficient of correlation r, also known as Pearson's coefficient, is a value that varies from −1 to 1. Correlation values equalling −1 or 1 present the condition where there is a perfect linear relationship, although in the real world, it is impossible to get a perfect linear relationship.

When this correlation value is computed with the help of statistical tools like Statistical Package for the Social Sciences (SPSS), Excel, or Stata, a p-value accompanies the figure. In line with other statistical tests, the p-value is used to infer whether the coefficient of correlation is statistically significant or not. This means determining whether a meaningful connection or association exists between the variables that can be relied upon for analysis and decision-making.

Points to note:

1. As r gets closer to zero, the strength of the linear relationship between variables becomes weaker.

2. The direction of the linear relationship between variables is determined based on the sign of the coefficient of correlation (or correlation coefficient). A positive correlation coefficient shows that variables have a positive linear relationship. An increase in one variable corresponds to an increase in the other variable.

3. In addition, a negative correlation coefficient usually points towards an inverse correlation between the variables. This involves a situation where when one of the variables goes up, the other variable goes down, or vice versa.

4. A perfect correlation is attained when the correlation coefficient is ±1. It is impossible to attain a perfect correlation.

5. The probability or *p*-value accompanying the test is used to test the significance of the linear relationship between variables. The p-value is compared against the conventional 5% level of significance when testing for the significance of the linear relationship between variables.

6. A correlation coefficient $r = 0$ implies a lack of linear relationship between variables.

To complete our interpretation of the coefficient of correlation, we need to test the significance and determine whether it can be relied upon for analysis and decision-making. Let's learn how to do this in the upcoming section.

7.3 Testing the Significance of the Correlation Coefficient

One may wish to determine if the correlation coefficient, ρ, is statistically significant. This assessment helps establish if there is a significant linear relationship between variables. A one-sample t-test is used to determine whether the observed correlation between two variables is statistically significant or if it could have occurred by chance.

To test for the significance of the correlation coefficient, ρ, the two-tailed test (explained in Chapter Nine, Section 9.4) is performed with the following hypotheses:

Null Hypothesis: H_0: $\rho = 0$

Alternative Hypothesis: H_a: $\rho \neq 0$

The test is computed with the formula:

$t = r\sqrt{\dfrac{n-2}{1-r^2}}$ given that $t \sim t_{\alpha/2,\ n-2}$ and r is the coefficient of

correlation

> The calculated t is compared to the critical t value obtained from the "Critical values of the t distribution table" added under the "Statistical Tables" section at the end of the book.

Decision: Reject the null hypothesis (H_0) if the calculated t value $\geq$ critical t value from the "Critical values of the t distribution table," otherwise do not reject.

Consequently, the probability values (p-values) that are automatically generated from statistical software can also be used to test the significance of the correlation coefficient. It entails comparing the obtained p-value to the set significance level.

Rejecting the null hypothesis leads to the conclusion that the correlation coefficient between the two variables is significant.

We will use the following example to illustrate our learnings from this chapter:

Example: Temperature and ice cream sales

Consider the data provided below of average temperature recordings on a given day and the total ice cream sales.

Table 7.2	Average temperature recordings and total ice cream sales

Temperature (°C)	14.2 16.4 11.9 15.2 18.5 22.1 19.4 25.1 23.4 18.1 22.6 17.2
Ice cream sales ($)	215 325 185 332 406 522 412 614 544 421 445 408

a. Determine the correlation coefficient between temperature and ice cream sales.

This can be achieved in Excel using the CORREL Function as shown below:

=CORREL(A1:M1,A2:M2)

Figure 7.3	Correlation coefficient between temperature and ice cream sales

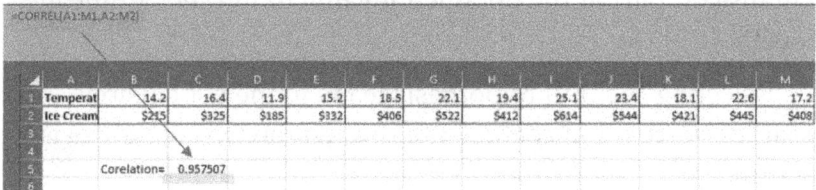

The correlation coefficient between average temperature and ice cream sales, $r = 0.957507$.

b. What can you say about the relationship between average temperature and ice cream sales?

The value of the correlation coefficient, r, is strong and positive. Higher average temperatures are associated with high ice cream sales and vice versa.

C. Is the relationship between average temperature and ice cream sales statistically significant at 5% level of significance?

To test the significance of the correlation coefficient, the following hypothesis is tested:

Null Hypothesis: $H_0: \rho = 0$

Alternative Hypothesis: $H_a: \rho \neq 0$

The test statistic is computed using the formula:

$t = r\sqrt{\dfrac{n-2}{1-r^2}}$ given that $t \sim t_{\alpha/2,\ n-2}$ and r is the coefficient of correlation.

The coefficient of correlation, $r = 0.957507$, and $n = 12$.

$t = r\sqrt{\dfrac{n-2}{1-r^2}} = 0.957507\sqrt{\dfrac{12-2}{1-0.957507^2}}$

$t = 10.4986$

The next step is to compare the calculated t-statistic to the critical t value from the "Critical values of the t distribution table" added under the "Statistical Tables" section at the end of the book.

The t critical value at a 5% significance level and 10 degrees of freedom ($n-2$) is 2.228.

| Figure 7.4 | Critical values of the t distribution table |

Table A. 2
t Distribution: Critical Values of *t*

Degrees of freedom	Two-tailed test: One-tailed test:	10% 5%	5% 2.5%	2% 1%	1% 0.5%	0.2% 0.1%	0.1% 0.05%
				Significance level			
1		6.314	12.706	31.821	63.657	318.309	636.619
2		2.920	4.303	6.965	9.925	22.327	31.599
3		2.353	3.182	4.541	5.841	10.215	12.924
4		2.132	2.776	3.747	4.604	7.173	8.610
5		2.015	2.571	3.365	4.032	5.893	6.869
6		1.943	2.447	3.143	3.707	5.208	5.959
7		1.894	2.365	2.998	3.499	4.785	5.408
8		1.860	2.306	2.896	3.355	4.501	5.041
9		1.833	2.262	2.821	3.250	4.297	4.781
10		1.812	2.228	2.764	3.169	4.144	4.587

When compared to the critical *t* value, the computed *t* value is greater. Therefore, the null hypothesis is rejected. A decision is made that the correlation coefficient is different from zero, i.e., it is statistically significant at the 5% level of significance.

7.3.1 Scatter plot

Besides calculating the correlation coefficient, we might be interested in visualizing the relationship between variables. To do this, a scatter plot is used. A scatter plot can also be referred to as a scatter diagram or scatter graph. Here, one of the variables is represented on the X axis and the other variable on the Y axis.

In this case, the variables are represented by numerical values, with dots used to identify them. If the dots are located near each other and have a trend to join in one straight line, then there is a high correlation between them. However, if the dots are far apart, the correlation between two variables is low.

Scatter plots are used in business to forecast sales, where a company may plot advertising spend vs. revenue to determine if higher marketing investments lead to increased sales. In customer analytics, businesses use scatter plots to analyze the correlation between customer satisfaction scores and retention rates, helping improve service strategies. Once patterns, clusters, or outliers are revealed from the scatter plots, businesses are enabled to make data-driven decisions.

Let's understand the types of correlation demonstrated by a scatter plot example:

1. **Negative correlation:** Here, a downward trend indicates that as one variable increases, the other decreases.

Figure 7.5 **Negative correlation**

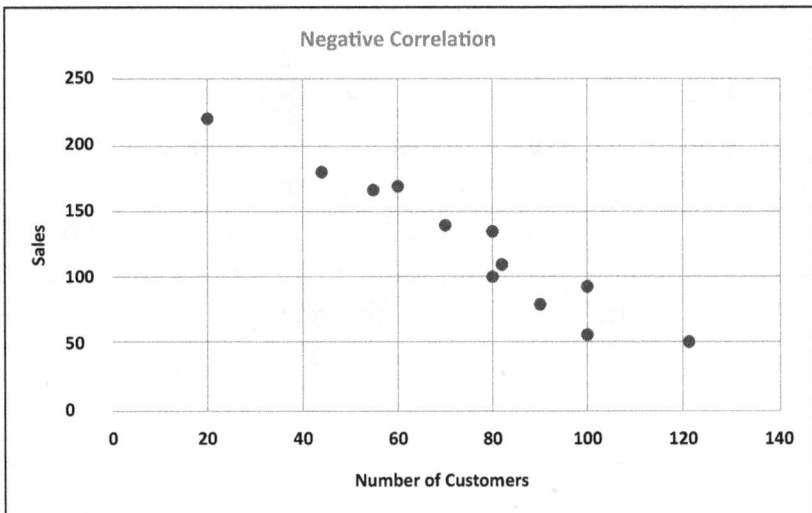

The plot shows that a few customers are associated with higher sales.

2. **Positive correlation:** Here, an upward trend indicates that as one variable increases, the other also increases.

Figure 7.6 Positive correlation

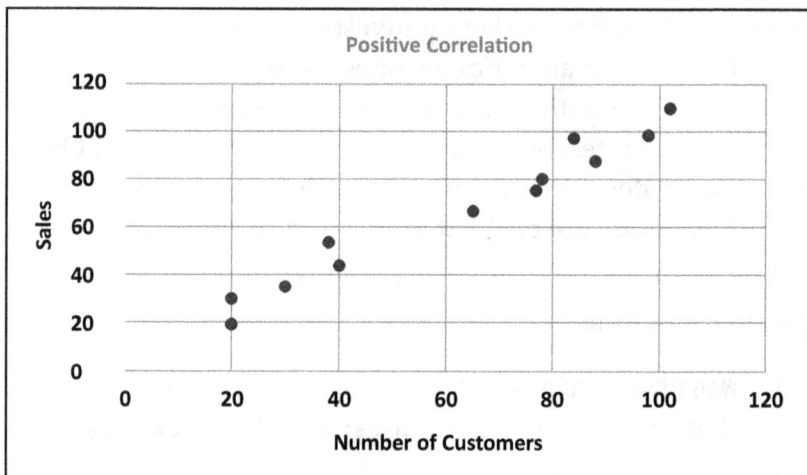

Here, the plot shows that high sales are associated with a higher number of customers.

3. **Weak Correlation:**

- The data points are widely scattered and do not closely follow a clear line or curve.
- There is a general trend (upward or downward), but it is hard to distinguish without statistical measures like the correlation coefficient.

Figure 7.7 Weak Correlation

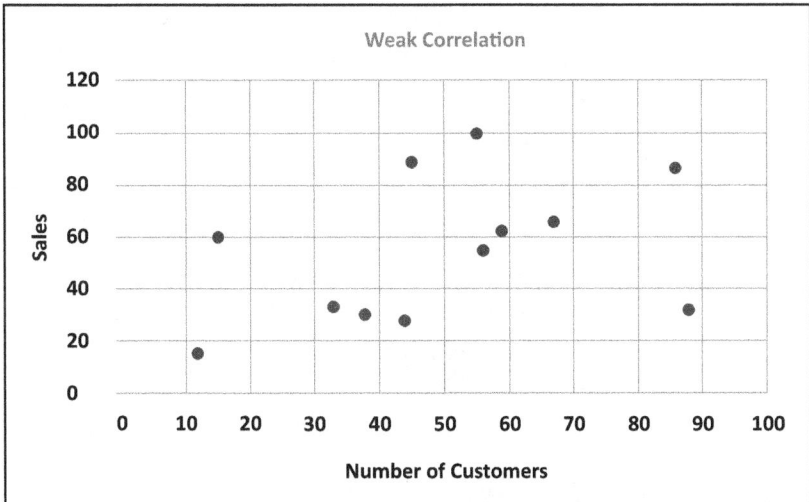

The plot shows that the relationship between sales and the number of customers is not strong, as shown by the sparse points.

7.4 Limitations of Correlation

While correlation is a useful statistical tool for measuring the strength and direction of relationships between variables, it has several limitations that can lead to misinterpretation of results.

1. A correlation can only be obtained in a bivariate dataset, involving two variables at a time.

2. The coefficient of correlation obtained from a test is affected by the presence of outliers in the data.

3. Correlation analysis is limited to linear relationships between variables.

4. Correlation does not account for causality.

In this chapter, we explored the fundamental concepts and limitations of correlation, learning how to measure the relationship between variables and interpret the values of the correlation coefficient. We also examined the process of testing the significance of these relationships and visualizing them effectively through scatter plots.

These skills enable us to identify and understand associations between variables, providing a strong foundation for data analysis. With this knowledge, we now transition to regression, where we will delve deeper into modeling and predicting relationships, moving from simple associations to causative insights.

Chapter Summary

- Correlation is a statistical method that establishes or identifies the magnitude of associations, as well as the direction of the relationship between variables.

- The Excel function =CORREL() returns the correlation coefficient between a pair of variables.

- The direction of the linear relationship between variables is determined based on the sign of the coefficient of correlation (or correlation coefficient). A positive correlation coefficient shows that variables have a positive linear relationship. An increase in one variable corresponds to an increase in the other variable.

- Correlation coefficient values range from −1 to +1.

- There is no linear relationship between a pair of variables if the correlation coefficient is zero.

- A scatter plot/scatter graph is a graphical representation of the linear relationship between variables.

- Correlation does not imply causation.

Further Learning

(Links also available in Online Resources)

1. **Correlation and regression**
   http://bit.ly/3UAzFKD
2. **Types of correlation**
   http://bit.ly/4lvJZhV
3. **Correlation analysis**
   http://bit.ly/3HI15vh

Quiz

1. **Consider the following correlations (*r*). Pick the strongest among them.**

   a. −0.54
   b. 0.50
   c. −0.44

Please note: The data below in Table 7.3 is an extract of the sales for two products, A and B. The number of customers served is also available, as shown. Answer questions 2–5 based on this data. (Detailed solution included in Online Resources.)

Table 7.3   **Sales of products A and B**

Customers	44	86	56	55	98	87	67	59	38	55	120	77
Sales (A)	27	86	75	23	67	56	66	43	87	76	75	41
Sales (B)	28	87	99	100	87	100	33	62	30	15	155	66

2. **Determine the correlation coefficient between the number of customers and the sales made for the twelve days for product B.**

   a. −0.86
   b. 0.745
   c. 0.867

3. **What is the interpretation of the correlation coefficient above?**

   a. The correlation is perfect and positive.
   b. The correlation is strong and positive.
   c. The correlation is weak and positive.

4. **Which products' sales are highly correlated with the number of customers who visited the store?**

   a. Sales for product A are highly correlated with the number of customers who visited the store, $r = -0.7446$, compared to sales for product B, $r = 0.2457$.

   b. Sales for product B are highly correlated with the number of customers who visited the store, $r = 0.7446$, compared to sales for product A, $r = 0.2457$.

   c. Sales for product B are highly correlated with the number of customers who visited the store, $r = -0.8676$, compared to sales for product A, $r = 0.2457$.

5. **Can it be concluded that a high number of customers on any day caused low sales for product A?**

   d. Yes, correlation and causation are one and the same.

   e. No, correlation between the number of customers served and the sales does not necessarily mean that there is causation between them.

   f. No, a high number of customers were served yet there were low sales.

6. **The scatter plot below shows how the price of a product changes with the demanded quantity.**

Figure 7.8   Supply curve

Determine the possible correlation coefficient between the sales and the quantity of the product.

   a.   0.31
   b.   −0.87
   c.   0.96

7.   **What is your reason for the answer above?**

   a.   There is a strong positive linear relationship between quantity and price of the commodity. As demand increases, the price of the commodity also increases.
   b.   There is a strong inverse linear relationship between quantity and price of the commodity. An increase in the demand is associated with a decrease in the price of the commodity.
   c.   Impossible to tell from the scatter plot.

Please note: A statistical software produced the following results when testing for the correlation between the age of an employee and their productivity. Answer the questions 8-10 below. (Detailed solution included in Online Resources.)

Figure 7.9   Correlation between age and productivity

Correlations

		Age of employee	Productivity
Age of employee	Pearson Correlation	1	.144
	Sig. (2-tailed)		.218
	N	75	75
Productivity	Pearson Correlation	.144	1
	Sig. (2-tailed)	.218	
	N	75	75

The Pearson Correlation is the same as the coefficient of correlation r

8. **Comment on the correlation coefficient between the age and productivity of an employee.**

   a. The correlation is positive but strong.
   b. The correlation is positive but weak.
   c. The correlation is positive but moderate.

9. **In testing the significance of the correlation coefficient, what is the null hypothesis?**

   a. The correlation coefficient is less than or equal to 0.05.
   b. The correlation coefficient is zero, i.e., not significant.
   c. The correlation coefficient is less than zero.

10. **What conclusion can be made given the results from the statistical software?**

   a. The linear relationship between age and productivity of an employee is statistically significant at $\alpha = 0.05$.

   b. The linear relationship between age and productivity of an employee is not statistically significant at $\alpha = 0.05$.

   c. The linear relationship between age and productivity of an employee is statistically significant at $\alpha = 0.01$.

Answers

1 – a	2 – b	3 – b	4 – b	5 – b
6 – c	7 – a	8 – b	9 – b	10 – b

CHAPTER 8

Regression Analysis

Key Learning Objectives

- Understand the fundamentals of regression analysis.
- Identify key assumptions of linear regression.
- Explore the concept of simple linear regression.
- Apply techniques for fitting a simple linear regression model.
- Learn about the coefficient of determination.
- Gain insight into multiple linear regression.

In the previous chapter, we discussed the concept of correlation—a measure of the strength and direction of the relationship between two variables. Correlation helps us understand the association between variables, however, it cannot be used to make predictions or quantify how one variable changes in response to another. At this point, regression analysis becomes essential.

This chapter builds upon the foundation of correlation by modeling the relationship between variables. It enables us to predict outcomes and uncover insights that are critical for organizations. You will be introduced to regression techniques, starting with simple linear regression and followed by multiple linear regression, which will equip you in both business and professional domains.

8.1 Introduction to Regression Analysis

On many occasions in the business environment, we need to establish an association or relationship between economic variables such as demand, supply, price, profits, discount, or loss. As we have seen, scatter plots are commonly utilized to visualize such relationships.

Alternatively, correlation analysis is useful in determining the magnitude and direction between variables. However, correlation does not imply causation. Correlation does not talk about the complex relationship between variables beyond the magnitude and direction of the variables.

Regression analysis provides a more formal and complex relationship between variables. In regression analysis, researchers model the relationship between variables by examining the impact of one or more variables on another. The variables that are thought to be impacting another variable are referred to as independent effects, predictors, explanatory variables, or X variables. The variables impacted or influenced by independent variables are known as the dependent or Y, response, or output variables.

The point at which the regression line crosses the y-axis is known as the intercept in regression analysis. The intercept, which sets the model's baseline and offers context for evaluating the slope coefficients, is crucial even though it is occasionally disregarded. Early comprehension of the intercept aids readers in understanding the entire regression equation.

Regression can also help in predicting the values of the output variable. Regression models created through predictive modeling are used to forecast values by analyzing various levels and quantities of input variables. Professionals use this analysis to determine possible future values of the response variable. Various combinations of the input variables can arrive at a combination of factors that optimize a certain response. In business settings, predictive modeling is used to keep the right inventory, make informed decisions, control risks, enhance customer insights, and gain a competitive advantage.

The knowledge gained through regression modeling can also help design and refine economic processes such as price determination, demand forecasting, inflation modeling, and labor market analysis.

Example

Imagine a retail chain owner who wants to know what factors significantly impact weekly sales performance in his stores. The owner collects data from 40 stores. The data collected has information on store size, number of employees, average foot traffic, and the amount spent on local advertising for each store. The owner suspects that these factors impact weekly sales.

In this problem, the objective is to model weekly sales. By using regression analysis, the chain can build a statistical model to link these predictors to weekly sales. This enables the owner to uncover actionable insights to improve store profitability and optimize resource allocation.

Generally, regression can be defined as the statistical technique or techniques used to estimate or quantify the relationship between factors. These factors can be either independent or dependent.

There are various types of regression. They include:

1. Linear regression
2. Logistic regression
3. Polynomial regression
4. Curvilinear regression

8.2 Linear Regression

In this chapter, we will focus only on the linear type of regression. Linear regression is often the starting point in regression analysis due to its simplicity, interpretability, and wide range of applications. Unlike other types of regression, it provides a straightforward method to understand relationships between variables and make predictions while requiring minimal computational effort.

There are two types of linear regression:

1. Simple linear regression
2. Multiple linear regression

8.2.1 Assumptions of the linear regression

To execute linear regression correctly, one needs to understand the assumptions underlying the technique. They include the following:

1. There should be a linear relationship between the dependent and the independent variable(s) when using linear regression, because the method is only valid

when the relationship follows a straight-line pattern. This means that when plotted on a graph, the data points should form a straight line, indicating a constant rate of increase or decrease between the variables. This is commonly known as the assumption of linearity, which can be tested using scatter plots.

2. Independent variables in the regression should not have high multicollinearity. High multicollinearity is problematic in multiple linear regression because it affects the stability and interpretability of the model. A high correlation between variables refers to a correlation coefficient value from 0.800 to 1.0.

3. The residual term, ϵ, follows the normal distribution with a mean of (0) as well as a variance of (σ^2). The Q-Q plots or tests, such as the test for normality of the residuals using the Shapiro–Wilk test, can be implemented.

4. There should be an independence of observations — data points should be unrelated to each other. This is important to obtain unbiased estimates as well as to increase the reliability of the regression model.

5. The error term and the independent variables should not be correlated. This is the endogeneity assumption. The assumption ensures that the estimated coefficients in a regression model are unbiased and reliable. Violating this assumption can lead to inconsistent estimates, making it difficult to determine the true relationship between variables.

8.2.2 Simple linear regression

A simple linear regression is a linear regression involving only one independent variable and one dependent variable. Generally, the equation is given as:

$$Y = \beta_0 + \beta_1 X + \epsilon$$

Where:

- Y is the outcome, dependent, or response variable.
- X is the independent variable.
- β_0 is the constant term or the intercept.
- β_1 is the coefficient of the independent variable or the slope.
- ϵ is the residual or the error term.

The simple linear regression equation/ line can be obtained using the "least squares method" or by use of statistical software.

Fitting a simple linear regression using the least squares method:

It is a technique used to solve linear regression problems by fitting the line of best fit to a set of data values. A line of best fit is a line that goes roughly through the middle of all the scatter points on a scatter plot. The closer the points are on a straight line, the stronger the association/ relationship between the variables plotted on the graph and vice versa.

The least squares regression method works by reducing the residuals to zero. The goal is to come up with a regression line in the form of $Y = \beta_0 + \beta_1 X + \epsilon$. The residual term, ϵ, in the equation is assumed to be zero. The least squares regression line can be fitted by using the formulas below to calculate the slope β_0 and the intercept β_1.

$$\beta_0 = \frac{N\sum(xy) - \sum x \sum y}{N\sum(x^2) - (\sum x)^2}$$

$$\beta_1 = \frac{\sum y - \beta0 \sum x}{N}$$

Example: Consider a business that wants to forecast the price of an item (Y dependent variable) based on demand (X independent variable). The following data has been collected for analysis.

| Table 8.1 | Price versus demand |

Demand (X)	125	120	130	160	320	350
Price ($) (Y)	25	36	45	33	44	56

| Table 8.2 | Least squares method |

Demand (X)	Price ($) (Y)	XY	X^2
125	25	3125	15625
120	36	4320	14400
130	45	5850	16900
160	33	5280	25600
320	44	14080	102400
350	56	19600	122500
Sum 1205	239	52255	297425

$$\beta_0 = \frac{N\sum(xy) - \sum x \sum y}{N\sum(x^2) - (\sum x)^2} = \frac{6(52255) - 1205^*239}{6(297425) - (1205)^2} = \frac{25,535}{332,525} = 0.07679$$

$$\beta_1 = \frac{\sum y - \beta 0 \sum x}{N} = \frac{239 - 0.07679^*1205}{6} = 24.41134$$

The regression line obtained using the least squares method is:

Price ($) = 0.07679 + 24.41134*Demand

The regression equation above can be interpreted as follows:

1. **Slope (β_0 = 0.07679):** It is the price of the item when the demand is zero. In the above problem, the price of the item when demand is zero is $0.07679.

2. **Intercept (β_1 = 24.41134):** A one-unit increase in the demand leads to a 24.41134 unit increase in the item's price.

A scatter plot can also be produced to visualize the changes in the price of the item with varying levels of demand, as shown below.

Figure 8.1 **Price vs. demand chart**

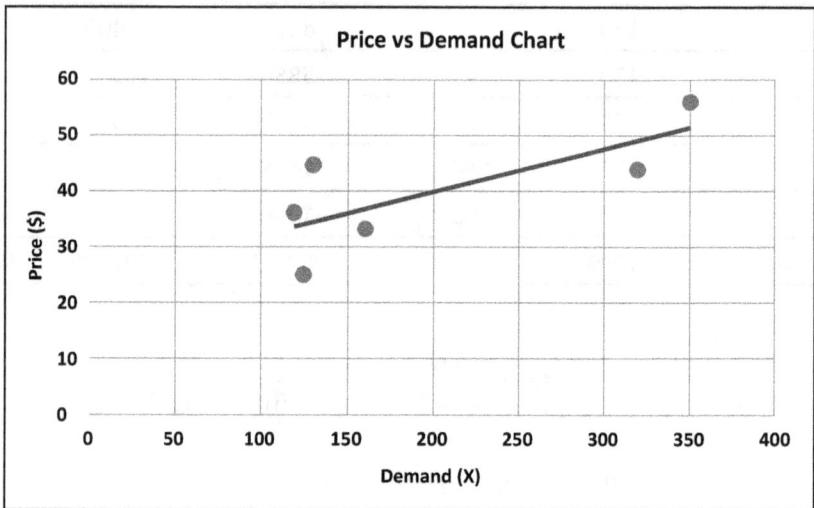

Coefficient of determination:

The coefficient of determination is referred to as the "R-squared." It is the percentage of variance in the dependent variable that can be explained by the independent or explanatory variable. As from the price and demand example discussed in the previous section, it depicts the extent to which the change in the dependent variable, that is "price," can be accounted for by the independent variable "demand."

Note that:

- The square of the correlation coefficient between the dependent and the independent variable gives the coefficient of determination in a simple linear regression.

- The range of the R-squared is 0 to 1.

- The response variable cannot be predicted if the R-squared value is 0.

- The response variable can be predicted accurately without error if the R-squared value is 1.

- The R-squared can be interpreted in terms of a percentage. For instance, an R-squared value of 0.89 implies that the independent variable accounts for 89% of the variance in the dependent variable.

The price and demand problem can also be solved using statistical software. In "Excel," a regression can be performed by clicking "Data," choosing "Data Analysis," and then selecting "Regression" as the analysis.

The solution to the price and demand problem in Excel is as follows:

Figure 8.2   The solution of the price and demand problem in Excel

SUMMARY OUTPUT

Regression Statistics	
Multiple R	0.746260919
R Square	0.556905359
Adjusted R Square	0.446131699
Standard Error	8.062609768
Observations	6

ANOVA

	df	SS	MS	F	Significance F
Regression	1	326.8106283	326.8106283	5.02741679	0.088406974
Residual	4	260.0227051	65.00567626		
Total	5	586.8333333			

	Coefficients	Standard Error	t Stat	P-value	Lower 95%	Upper 95%	Lower 95.0%	Upper 95.0%
Intercept	24.41109691	7.625217298	3.2013641	0.032858059	3.240099667	45.58209415	3.240099667	45.58209415
Demand (X)	0.076791219	0.034248308	2.242190177	0.088406974	-0.018297327	0.171879764	-0.018297327	0.171879764

- Multiple R: The correlation between the dependent and the independent variables.
- The R-squared value is the coefficient of determination.
- The Analysis of Variance (ANOVA) table is used when testing the overall significance of the model. It includes the F-statistic, which measures the ratio of the variation explained by the model (Mean Square Regression, MSR) to the variation that remains unexplained (Mean Square Error, MSE or residual).
- A higher F-value indicates that the model explains a significant portion of the variation in the dependent variable. The F-statistic is accompanied by a p-value, which helps determine whether the model is statistically significant. If the p-value is less than a chosen significance level (e.g., 0.05), we reject the null hypothesis and conclude that the model is meaningful.

8.2.3 Multiple linear regression

A multiple linear regression involves performing a linear regression with two or more independent variables. In the "price and demand" problem seen in the previous section, only one independent variable was used. The business may want to add other factors, such as the cost of production. The problem thus becomes a multiple linear regression.

Generally, a multiple linear regression is expressed as:

$Y = \beta_0 + \beta_1 X_1 + \beta_2 X_2 + \ldots + \beta_n X_n + \epsilon$, where n is the number of predictor variables in the model.

Let's assume that we have the data on the cost of production of the item as shown in Table 8.3 below:

Table 8.3   Cost of production

Demand	120	230	300	160	320	400
Price ($)	25	36	45	33	44	56
Cost of Production ($)	20	30	38	33	42	44

The output of the multiple linear regression computed using Excel is given in Figure 8.3 below.

Figure 8.3   The output of the multiple linear regression

SUMMARY OUTPUT

Regression Statistics	
Multiple R	0.930669758
R Square	0.866146199
Adjusted R Square	0.776910331
Standard Error	5.116961092
Observations	6

ANOVA

	df	SS	MS	F	Significance F
Regression	2	508.2834609	254.1417304	9.706256261	0.0489718
Residual	3	78.54987246	26.18329082		
Total	5	586.8333333			

	Coefficients	Standard Error	t Stat	P-value	Lower 95%	Upper 95%	Lower 95.0%	Upper 95.0%
Intercept	1.462035002	9.97030821	0.146638897	0.892716776	-30.26793552	33.19200553	-30.26793552	33.19200553
Demand (X)	0.007695336	0.034077598	0.225818028	0.83585278	-0.10075479	0.116145462	-0.10075479	0.116145462
Cost of production	1.067415025	0.405452159	2.63265345	0.078146875	-0.2229147	2.35774475	-0.2229147	2.35774475

Adding the cost of production as a predictor for price alters the original regression model. The new regression model, which is a multivariate linear regression, is given as:

Price ($) = 1.4620 + 0.00769*Demand + 1.0674*Cost of production

The figures are taken from the output above. The intercept (β_0) is 1.4620, the coefficient for Demand (β_1) is 0.00769, while the coefficient for cost of production (β_2) is 1.0674.

Interpretation:

- **Intercept:** The price of the item is $1.4620 when the demand and cost of production are zero.
- **Coefficient for demand:** A one-unit increase in demand for the item, holding the cost of production constant, increases the price of the item by 0.00769 units.
- **Coefficient of the cost of production:** A one-unit increase in the cost of production for the item, holding the demand constant, increases the price of the item by 1.0674 units.

The R-squared (coefficient of determination) is 0.8661, which implies that the predictor variables (demand and cost of production) account for approximately 86.61% of the variance in the dependent variable (price).

Adding the cost of production as a predictor variable contributed to an increase in the proportion of variance of price explained by the model. In the simple linear model (output shown in Fig. 8.2), we saw that demand as the only predictor variable accounted for only 55.6% (R square = 0.556 from the simple linear regression). Therefore, the addition of the cost of production improved the model.

The overall significance of the model is tested using the ANOVA model. The F statistic is tested by comparing the significance value of F against a specified level of significance.

Let us consider the following example to help us summarize all the concepts that we have covered under multivariate regression analysis.

Example

An importer in California wants to know the factors that determine the average price of Honda vehicles imported from Japan. The following data is collected for analysis.

Table 8.4 The average price, import tariff, and shipping fee

Average Price ($)	Import tariff ($)	Shipping fee ($)
140	60	22
155	62	25
159	67	24
179	70	20
192	71	15
200	72	14
212	75	14
215	78	11

1. Determine the correlation between the average price of a Honda vehicle and the shipping fee. Interpret it.

2. Fit a multiple linear regression and interpret it.

3. Use the output generated to test the significance of the coefficients of the predictor variables (use a 5% significance level). The concept of significance levels is explained further under Chapter Nine, Section 9.4.1.

4. Identify and explain the value of the coefficient of determination.

5. Test the overall significance of the regression model (use a 5% significance level).

Solution:

1. Determining correlation:

Figure 8.4 Correlation between the average price of a Honda vehicle and shipping fee

| | File | Home | Insert | Draw | Page Layout | Formulas | Data | Review | View | Developer | H |

D4   ✕ ✓ *fx*   =CORREL(B4:B11,D4:D11)

▲	A	B	C	D	E	F	G	H	I	J
1										
2										
3		Price ($)	Import tariff ($)	Shipping fee ($)		Correlation	=CORREL(B4:B11,D4:D11)			
4		140	60	22						
5		155	62	25						
6		159	67	24						
7		179	70	20						
8		192	71	15						
9		200	72	14						
10		212	75	14						
11		215	78	11						
12										

The correlation coefficient between the average price of a Honda vehicle and the shipping fee is −0.9259.

The correlation is negative and strong. The relationship is inverse, indicating that as the average price of Honda vehicles increases, the shipping fee tends to decrease and vice versa.

2. Multiple linear regression equation:

| Figure 8.5 | Output |

SUMMARY OUTPUT

Regression Statistics	
Multiple R	0.981130154
R Square	0.96261638
Adjusted R Square	0.947662932
Standard Error	6.378740646
Observations	8

ANOVA

	df	SS	MS	F	Significance F
Regression	2	5238.558339	2619.279169	64.37420819	0.000270211
Residual	5	203.4416611	40.68833222		
Total	7	5442			

	Coefficients	Standard Error	t Stat	P-value	Lower 95%	Upper 95%	Lower 95.0%	Upper 95.0%
Intercept	-6.867487248	74.31203997	-0.092414194	0.929957505	-197.8926674	184.1576929	-197.8926674	184.1576929
Import tariff ($)	3.147893103	0.838692746	3.753332933	0.01324815	0.991964765	5.30382144	0.991964765	5.30382144
Shipping fee ($)	-1.656143269	0.975941859	-1.696969193	0.150463535	-4.164881684	0.852595146	-4.164881684	0.852595146

The regression model from the output is:

Price (\$) = −6.8675 + 3.14789*import tariff −1.6561*shipping fee

The figures are taken from the output above. The intercept (β_0) is −6.8675, the coefficient for Import tariff (β_1) is 3.14789, while the coefficient for shopping fee (β_2) is −1.6561.

3. Interpreting coefficients:

A. **Coefficient of the import tariff:** A one-dollar increase in the import tariff, holding the shipping fee constant, increases the average price of a Honda vehicle by \$3.14789.

B. **Coefficient of the shipping fee:** A one-dollar increase in shipping fee, holding the import tariff constant, decreases the average price of a Honda vehicle by \$1.6561.

204 / Business Statistics Essentials

Testing the significance of the coefficients of the predictor variables:

Coefficient of the import tariff: 3.14789.

The p-value for the coefficient of the import tariff is $p = 0.01324$. The coefficient is significant at a 5% significance level.

Coefficient of the shipping fee tariff: -1.65614.

The p-value for the coefficient of the shipping fee is $p = 0.15046$. The coefficient is not significant at a 5% significance level.

4. Coefficient of determination:

The coefficient of determination (R-squared) for the model is 0.9626. The model accounts for 96.26% of the variance in the average price of a Honda vehicle.

5. Testing the significance of the model:

The model has a test statistic $F (2, 5) = (64.3742, p < 0.001)$. The model is significant at a 5% significance level.

With this example, we're at the end of Chapter Eight. In this chapter, we explored the essential concepts of regression, learning how to model and analyze relationships between variables using both simple and multiple linear regression techniques. We learnt how to fit regression models, evaluate their assumptions, and interpret key metrics such as the coefficient of determination.

These skills enable us to move beyond correlation, providing the tools to predict outcomes and make data-driven decisions. Equipped with this knowledge, we can confidently address complex problems, harnessing regression as a powerful tool for strategic insight and forecasting.

www.vibrantpublishers.com

Chapter Summary

- Regression analysis is used to model the relationship between variables by examining the impact of one variable(s) on another.

- Regression is useful in optimization, forecasting, and explaining the relationship between variables in detail.

- There are various types of regression. The most common type of regression is linear regression.

- There are two types of linear regression: Simple and multiple linear regression.

- Simple linear regression has only one independent variable, while multiple linear regression has two or more independent variables.

- The general equation for simple linear regression is $Y = \beta_0 + \beta_1 X + \epsilon$, while the general equation for multiple linear regression is $Y = \beta_0 + \beta_1 X_1 + \beta_2 X_2 + \ldots\ldots\ldots\ldots + \beta_n X_n + \epsilon$.

- The significance of regression models and regression coefficients can be tested using the test statistic generated and the p-values generated by statistical software.

Further Learning

(Links also available in Online Resources)

1. **Multiple linear regression**
http://bit.ly/45rX3jW

2. **Assumptions of multiple linear regression**
http://bit.ly/45XP8uI

3. **Difference between simple and multiple linear regression**
http://bit.ly/45peiCo

4. **Testing multiple linear regression coefficients**
http://bit.ly/4mqV8lE

Quiz

1. **What is the difference between regression and correlation?**

   a. Correlation and regression are one and the same.

   b. Correlation is used to determine if there is a linear relationship, the strength and direction; however, regression determines the complex nature of the relationship.

   c. Correlation implies causation, but regression does not.

2. **Define Regression.**

   a. Regression is a method used to select variables that are beneficial to a process.

   b. Regression is a statistical technique where the impact or effect of inputs on the output is determined.

   c. It is a statistical technique that can be used to test linear relationships between variables.

3. **Regression analysis is an important component in a business. All the following are the benefits of employing regression analysis in a business setup except one. Which one is it?**

   a. Predicting sales

   b. Forecasting demand

   c. Determining strategies used by competitors

4. **Define the coefficient of determination.**

   a. It is the proportion of variance in the independent variable explained by the dependent variable in a regression model.

   b. It is the proportion of variance in the dependent variable explained by the independent variables in a regression model.

   c. It refers to the number of independent variables in a regression model.

5. **Economists found that there is a perfect positive linear relationship between price and demand for a product. What could this mean?**

   a. Demand is the sole determinant of the price of the product.

   b. Demand is not the only determinant of the price of the product.

   c. There is an inverse association between demand and price.

6. **Which of the following is not an assumption of linear regression?**

   a. There should be a linear relationship between the dependent and the independent variable(s).

   b. There must be a perfect linear relationship between the dependent and the independent variables.

   c. The residual term, ϵ, follows a normal distribution with a mean of zero and variance (σ^2).

7. **Which is true about multicollinearity in regression analysis?**

   a. It occurs when the dependent variable in a regression model is highly correlated with one or more independent variables.

   b. It occurs when two or more independent variables are highly correlated in a regression model.

   c. It occurs when there is no linear relationship between the dependent and the independent variables in a regression model.

8. **A researcher tested two simple linear regression models to determine factors that influence the price (in dollars) of houses in real estate. The first model with the size of the houses (in square feet) yielded the model $Y = 250 + 0.245X_1$, while the second model with distance from the city (in miles) resulted in the model $Y = 231 + 0.548X_1$. Approximate the price from both models for a house that is 2000 square feet, using model 1, and a house that is 2050 miles from the city, using model 2. (Detailed solution included in Online Resources.)**

   a. $745 and $1400, respectively

   b. $740 and $1354.40, respectively

   c. $840 and $1500, respectively

9. **In question 8 above, the first model had an R-squared value of 0.561 while the second model had an R-squared value of 0.89. Between the size of the house and the distance from the city, which is a better predictor of the price of a house? (Detailed solution included in Online Resources.)**

   a. The size of the house.

   b. The distance from the city.

   c. There is no difference between the factors.

10. **Which statement is true about the simple linear and multiple linear regression?**

   a. A simple linear regression involves one categorical variable as the independent variable, while a multiple linear regression involves continuous variables as independent variables in a regression model.

   b. A multiple linear regression involves two or more independent variables, while a simple linear regression involves one independent variable.

   c. The coefficient of determination is higher for a multiple linear regression than for a simple linear regression.

Answers

1 – b	2 – b	3 – c	4 – b	5 – a
6 – b	7 – b	8 – b	9 – b	10 – b

CHAPTER 9

Hypothesis Testing

Key Learning Objectives

- Learn what a hypothesis means, sources of hypotheses, and types of errors (Types I & II).
- Explore significance level and confidence level.
- Study statistical testing and estimation.
- Determine the critical region in hypothesis testing.
- Conduct hypothesis testing for large and small samples.
- Explore real-world applications like A/B testing and quality control.

In the previous chapters, we have seen that data is the bedrock of business statistics. Data analysis informs decision-making. Thus, businesses need to have a systematic way of arriving at conclusions based on the collected and analyzed data.

Consider scenarios such as a business wanting to understand the impact training has had on the employees' productivity, weather conditions impacting the sale of ice cream on a given day, or determining if organizational culture influences the productivity of a firm. A systematic mechanism for arriving at conclusions on these activities must be determined. This is where hypothesis testing becomes invaluable.

Hypothesis testing builds on the foundations of descriptive statistics, probability, sampling, and regression analysis. It provides a formal method for evaluating assumptions or claims about a population based on sample data. It enables business professionals to make more confident, evidence-based decisions, minimizing risk and maximizing the likelihood of success.

This chapter will introduce you to hypothesis testing with real-world examples, procedures for testing a hypothesis, and drawing conclusions. It will equip you with the skills and ability to analyze data and substantiate business strategies.

9.1 Introduction to Hypothesis Testing

A hypothesis is an assumption, a proposition, or a claim about a particular phenomenon. A hypothesis may or may not be true. It is unverified and untested; researchers have the task of proving or validating it scientifically by obtaining and collecting data.

Hypothesis testing is the process of testing the assumptions, propositions, or claims about population parameters by collecting data from a sample, analyzing and making conclusions based on the results.

We have seen in previous chapters how statistics is important in a business environment, whether it is rolling out a new marketing strategy, determining the stocking quantities, selecting samples, or determining the impact of various factors on another factor. At this point, a researcher must confirm or test the claims or assumptions underlying every statistical application mentioned previously. For this purpose, the concept of hypothesis testing has become very handy.

A researcher needs to specify the null and alternative hypotheses before testing the hypotheses. A null hypothesis is an assumption, proposition, or claim that should be disproved or rejected. The alternative hypothesis is the assumption, proposition, or claim that a researcher wants to prove if there is enough evidence to reject the null hypothesis. H_0 denotes the null hypothesis, while H_a or H_1 denotes the alternative hypothesis.

At the end of testing a hypothesis, a decision must be made: either reject or fail to reject the null hypothesis. Rejecting a null hypothesis is an indication of the availability of sufficient evidence against it based on the analyzed sample data. Additionally, failing to reject the hypothesis does not translate into accepting it; rather, it means that there is not enough evidence from the data to reject it, and that the variations are attributed to chance or errors in sampling.

The main objective of a researcher is to reject the null hypothesis, subject to the availability of evidence.

Hypothesis testing is synonymous with a court trial. Imagine a suspect taken to court and charged. A judge has to decide whether the person is innocent (null hypothesis) or guilty (alternative hypothesis). Accusers must provide sufficient evidence for the judge to convict the suspected person otherwise, the person will be freed. Freeing the suspect does not mean that the suspect did not commit the crime. It means that there is insufficient evidence to convict the suspect.

In some cases, hypothesis testing may lead to incorrect decisions and conclusions, thus leading to errors. We will look into this in the following section.

9.2 Type I and II Errors

There are two types of errors in hypothesis testing:

1. Type I error
2. Type II error

A Type I error occurs if a null hypothesis is rejected when it is actually true. It is also known as a "false positive" conclusion. A type II error, also known as a false negative, is the decision to fail to reject the null hypothesis when it is not true.

We will understand type I and type II errors using the following example. It will help us identify these errors and make the correct decision in statistical hypothesis testing.

Scenario: A supermarket management wants to understand whether their new promotional campaign improved customer satisfaction ratings. Before the campaign, the average customer satisfaction rating was 70%. They asked their customers to give their ratings of satisfaction and analyzed the data.

From this scenario, the null and alternative hypotheses are stated as follows:

- **Null Hypothesis (H_0):** The new promotional campaign does not improve customer satisfaction ratings (average rating remains 70%).

- **Alternative Hypothesis (H₁):** The new promotional campaign improves customer satisfaction ratings (average score is greater than 70%).

The mechanism of type I and type II errors is outlined in Figure 9.1 below:

Types of errors

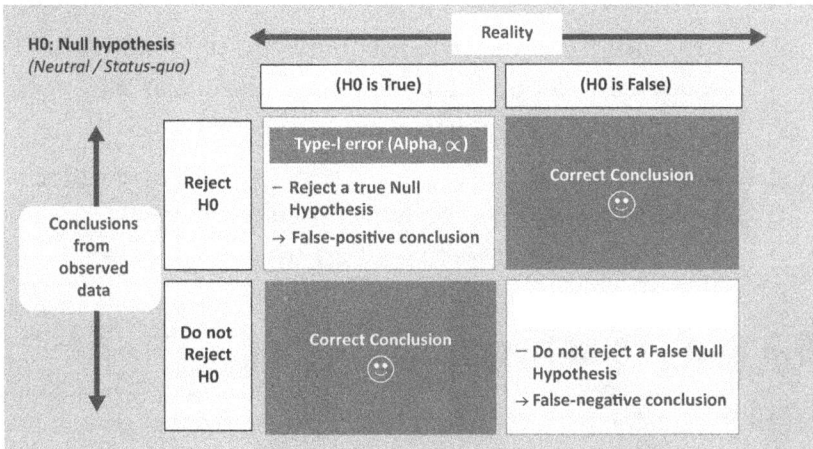

1. **Type I error (false positive)**

   A Type I error occurs when the supermarket rejects the null hypothesis even though the new promotional campaign does not improve customer satisfaction. In this case, the supermarket concludes that the new promotional campaign is effective, they invest more resources in expanding it, but ultimately realize no real improvement in customer satisfaction rating.

2. **Type II error (false negative)**

   A Type II error occurs when the supermarket fails to reject the null hypothesis even though the new promotional campaign does improve customer satisfaction. Here, the supermarket incorrectly concludes that the campaign is not effective, does away with it, and misses an opportunity to enhance its customer satisfaction rating.

Impact on business:

In each case of errors, the impact on the business is as follows:

1. **Type I error:** The supermarket may end up wasting resources and potentially losing credibility if the program fails to deliver promised results.

2. **Type II error:** The supermarket may miss an opportunity to capitalize on an effective strategy, potentially allowing competitors to gain an edge.

9.3 Sources of Hypothesis Testing

In the business world, statistical hypotheses can come from a number of sources, guiding data collection.

1. **Business problems and challenges**

    Most hypotheses arise from the identification of gaps in knowledge within businesses. These gaps often stem from real-world problems or strategic decisions that require empirical validation.

    For instance, a business may want to test the claim that a new marketing strategy increases sales by 20%. The claim may prompt the formulation of a hypothesis to determine whether the observed sales growth is statistically significant and directly attributable to the new strategy.

2. Theories and scientific principles

Researchers may want to test known theories, such as the theories of supply and demand, by collecting data. The conclusions may lead to validation or rejection of the theories.

3. Industry benchmarks and trends

Industry reports and analyses, competitor analysis, or general business trends in the industry are also primary sources of hypotheses. For instance, an e-commerce company may predict that increasing free shipping options will cause the conversion rate to be higher than what it is in similar companies.

4. Popular beliefs

Several popular beliefs are prevalent in the marketing domain. One example is the popular saying that "people buy on emotion, then justify with logic." Such beliefs spark questions that may require validation by collecting data and making an appropriate decision.

Having been introduced to hypotheses and the sources that may give rise to hypothesis testing, the next step is to conduct the hypothesis testing, as we will study in the upcoming Section 9.4.

But before that, there are some key concepts in hypothesis testing that we will need to understand. This will help us test hypotheses with confidence and make accurate statistical conclusions. Let us discuss these concepts in the upcoming section.

9.4 Key Concepts in Hypothesis Testing

Learning the following concepts will help us ensure statistical accuracy in our findings:

9.4.1 Significance levels and confidence levels

Significance levels and confidence levels are fundamental in quantifying uncertainty in statistical analysis. Let's understand what they mean:

1. **Significance level**

    It is the threshold upon which a decision to reject or failure to reject a null hypothesis is made. It also represents the probability of making a Type I error—rejecting the null hypothesis when it is actually true. The symbol α is used to denote a significance level. This level of significance must be specified in hypothesis testing as it is used to set the threshold for making a conclusion. The most applicable levels of significance are $\alpha = 0.05$, $\alpha = 0.01$, and $\alpha = 0.10$.

    Sometimes, a researcher may not know which level of significance to apply. In such cases a $\alpha = 0.05$ should be used as it is a conventional value for the significance level.

    The α can be interpreted as a percentage. A $\alpha = 0.05$ is equivalent to a 5% risk of rejecting the null hypothesis when it is true. It also represents a 5% chance of committing a Type I error by definition. Once a hypothesis test is done, the p-value from the analysis is compared against the specified level of significance. This leads to either rejecting or failing to reject the null hypothesis.

2. Confidence interval

In an analysis to obtain estimates, every researcher desires to get the same values of the estimate on redoing the analysis. A confidence level or interval is the interval in which estimates are expected to fall when the analysis is done with a certain confidence.

The confidence interval and the level of significance are complementary. To calculate the confidence level, the following formula is used:

$$\text{Confidence level} = 1 - \alpha$$

Take, for instance, $\alpha = 0.05$; the confidence interval is 0.95. A 0.95 confidence level shows that the researcher is 95% confident that an estimate will fall within the confidence interval.

9.4.2 Standard error and sampling error

A standard error is the measure of variability or the margin of error in the estimation of the population parameters from the sample statistic. It is also seen as the standard deviation of the sample statistic.

The standard error is important in hypothesis testing for the following reasons:

1. It aids in constructing confidence intervals. A small standard error means that the confidence interval will be narrow. However, as the standard error increases, so does the width of the confidence interval.

   $$\text{Confidence interval} = \text{sample mean} \pm (Z * \text{standard error})$$

   Z is the standard score obtained from the cumulative normal distribution tables attached at the end of the book.

2. The standard error is used to calculate test statistics, which we will discuss in the next section.

3. It is also used to estimate the extent of the variable of the sample estimate from the real population parameter.

A sampling error refers to the maximum allowable value that is attributed to deviations caused by chance in sampling. This error arises due to the natural variability that occurs when a sample, rather than the entire population, is used to estimate population characteristics.

Sampling error = Critical value of the test statistic at a specified level of significance - The standard error of the sample statistic.

9.4.3 Test statistic

It is the numerical value obtained from a test of sample data drawn from the population, and upon which a decision to reject or fail to reject the null hypothesis is made. Some statistical tests include the t-test, Z-test, F-test, Chi-square test, and the test for the correlation coefficient. These tests produce a numerical value known as the test statistic.

Test statistics are computed or applied depending on the nature of the data and the type of hypothesis being tested. Test statistics may be calculated manually or by statistical software.

> A hypothesis can be tested by calculating the appropriate test statistics and then comparing them to the critical value of the test. The critical values of each test statistic are added under the "Statistical Tables" section at the end of the book.

9.4.4 Critical region in hypothesis testing

A critical region, commonly referred to as the rejection region, is the region that contains all the values of the test statistic that lead to the rejection of the null hypothesis. Conversely, the set values of the test statistic that lead to failure to reject the null hypothesis constitute the acceptance region. These two regions help us define a critical value beyond which a decision is made to reject the null hypothesis.

An illustration of the critical region is shown below:

a) $\alpha = 0.05$

Figure 9.2 **The normal distribution curve (two-tailed test) for $\alpha = 0.05$**

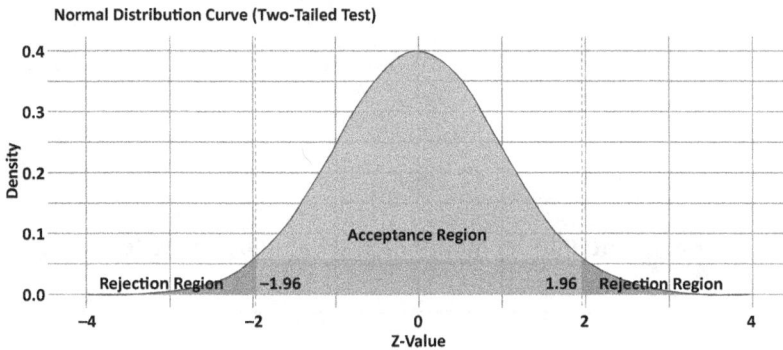

Normal Distribution Curve (Two-Tailed Test)

Rejection Region   −1.96   Acceptance Region   1.96   Rejection Region

Z-Value

Figure 9.3 **The normal distribution curve (one-tailed test) for $\alpha = 0.05$**

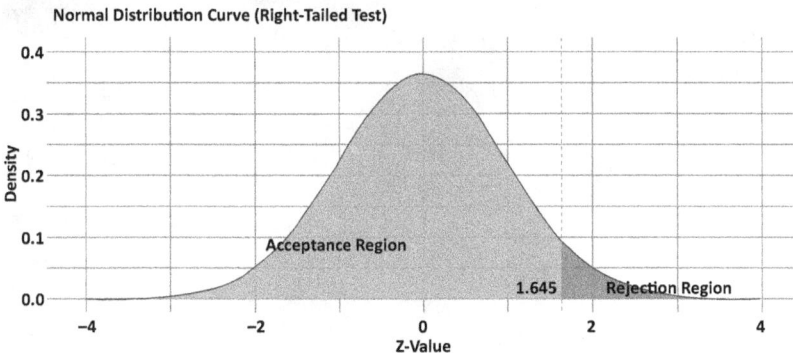

Normal Distribution Curve (Right-Tailed Test)

Acceptance Region   1.645   Rejection Region

Z-Value

b) $\alpha = 0.01$

Figure 9.4 The normal distribution curve (two-tailed test) for $\alpha = 0.01$

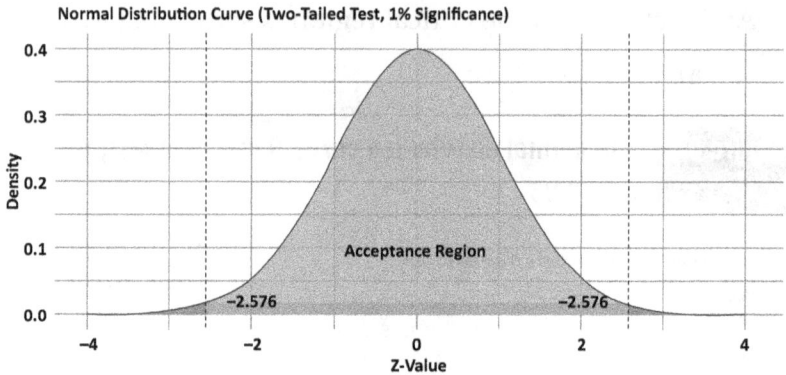

Normal Distribution Curve (Two-Tailed Test, 1% Significance)

Acceptance Region

−2.576   −2.576

Z-Value

Figure 9.5 The normal distribution curve (one-tailed test) for $\alpha = 0.05$

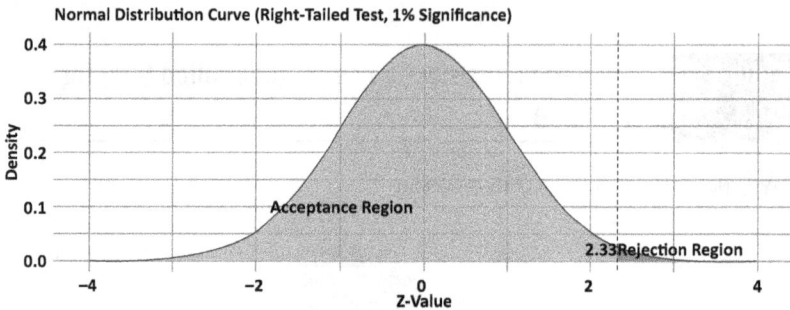

Normal Distribution Curve (Right-Tailed Test, 1% Significance)

Acceptance Region

2.33 Rejection Region

Z-Value

9.4.5 Determining the type of hypothesis

A hypothesis to test may be one-sided or two-sided, depending on the research question. Let us see how this occurs with the examples below:

1. **One-sided hypothesis**

   Think of a vendor who believes that she serves fewer than 67 customers in a day. We could test the vendor's belief by formulating the following hypothesis:

   Null hypothesis (H_0): The number of customers served was greater than or equal to 67 (this is the claim that should be disproved).

   Alternative hypothesis (H_a): The number of customers served is less than 67 (the claim that should be proved).

   A one-sided hypothesis deals with variations in one direction from the null hypothesis. In the hypothesis scenario specified above, the null hypothesis points to the number of customers served being greater than 67, while the alternative hypothesis points to the number of customers served being less than 67.

   Testing this hypothesis requires a one-tailed test. A one-tailed test may be right-tailed or left-tailed. It depends on the direction of the alternative hypothesis. In the case above, a left-tailed test will be conducted as the parameter of interest points to a direction where a smaller number of customers were served.

2. **Two-sided hypothesis**

   Suppose the vendor thinks that the number of customers served is different from 67, then the null and alternative hypotheses can be stated as below:

Null hypothesis (H_0): The number of customers served was 67.

Alternative hypothesis (H_a): The number of customers was not 67; the number of customers could be greater or less than 67.

This test is two-sided as the alternative hypothesis has two sides: either less than or greater than 67 customers served. This hypothesis will be tested using a two-tailed test.

9.4.6 Reading critical values of test statistics from statistical tables

Statistical tables provide critical values for all test statistics. These tables can be accessed using the internet. They have been added under the "Statistical Tables" section at the end of the book.

Let's learn how to read the critical values for some common statistical tests:

1. **Z table (the standard normal distribution)**

   The critical values of a Z-test can be obtained by reading the corresponding value of the level of significance (α) and the test (one-tailed or two-tailed). The Z table is used for large samples where $n \geq 30$. The critical value of Z for a one-tailed test at $\alpha = 0.05$ is 1.645 and ± 1.96 for a two-tailed test at $\alpha = 0.05$.

   To read the critical value, find the area in the table that corresponds to the desired significance level and alpha. For instance, to read the one-tailed Z value for $\alpha = 0.05$, we search for the value that corresponds to $1 - 0.05$, i.,e 0.95. However, we search for the value $1 - 0.025$, i.e, 0.975, for a two-tailed Z value because we divide α by two before subtracting it from 1. This is illustrated in Figure 9.6 below:

Figure 9.6 | The standardized normal distribution curve

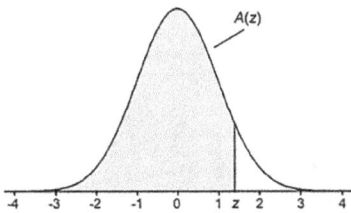

A(z) is the integral of the standardized normal distribution from $-\infty$ to z (in other words, the area under the curve to the left of z). It gives the probability of a normal random variable not being more than z standard deviations above its mean. Values of z of particular importance:

z	$A(z)$	
1.645	0.9500	Lower limit of right 5% tail
1.960	0.9750	Lower limit of right 2.5% tail
2.326	0.9900	Lower limit of right 1% tail
2.576	0.9950	Lower limit of right 0.5% tail
3.090	0.9990	Lower limit of right 0.1% tail
3.291	0.9995	Lower limit of right 0.05% tail

z	0.00	0.01	0.02	0.03	0.04	0.05	0.06	0.07	0.08	0.09
0.0	0.5000	0.5040	0.5080	0.5120	0.5160	0.5199	0.5239	0.5279	0.5319	0.5359
0.1	0.5398	0.5438	0.5478	0.5517	0.5557	0.5596	0.5636	0.5675	0.5714	0.5753
0.2	0.5793	0.5832	0.5871	0.5910	0.5948	0.5987	0.6026	0.6064	0.6103	0.6141
0.3	0.6179	0.6217	0.6255	0.6293	0.6331	0.6368	0.6406	0.6443	0.6480	0.6517
0.4	0.6554	0.6591	0.6628	0.6664	0.6700	0.6736	0.6772	0.6808	0.6844	0.6879
0.5	0.6915	0.6950	0.6985	0.7019	0.7054	0.7088	0.7123	0.7157	0.7190	0.7224
0.6	0.7257	0.7291	0.7324	0.7357	0.7389	0.7422	0.7454	0.7486	0.7517	0.7549
0.7	0.7580	0.7611	0.7642	0.7673	0.7704	0.7734	0.7764	0.7794	0.7823	0.7852
0.8	0.7881	0.7910	0.7939	0.7967	0.7995	0.8023	0.8051	0.8078	0.8106	0.8133
0.9	0.8159	0.8186	0.8212	0.8238	0.8264	0.8289	0.8315	0.8340	0.8365	0.8389
1.0	0.8413	0.8438	0.8461	0.8485	0.8508	0.8531	0.8554	0.8577	0.8599	0.8621
1.1	0.8643	0.8665	0.8686	0.8708	0.8729	0.8749	0.8770	0.8790	0.8810	0.8830
1.2	0.8849	0.8869	0.8888	0.8907	0.8925	0.8944	0.8962	0.8980	0.8997	0.9015
1.3	0.9032	0.9049	0.9066	0.9082	0.9099	0.9115	0.9131	0.9147	0.9162	0.9177
1.4	0.9192	0.9207	0.9222	0.9236	0.9251	0.9265	0.9279	0.9292	0.9306	0.9319
1.5	0.9332	0.9345	0.9357	0.9370	0.9382	0.9394	0.9406	0.9418	0.9429	0.9441
1.6	0.9452	0.9463	0.9474	0.9484	0.9495	0.9505	0.9515	0.9525	0.9535	0.9545
1.7	0.9554	0.9564	0.9573	0.9582	0.9591	0.9599	0.9608	0.9616	0.9625	0.9633
1.8	0.9641	0.9649	0.9656	0.9664	0.9671	0.9678	0.9686	0.9693	0.9699	0.9706
1.9	0.9713	0.9719	0.9726	0.9732	0.9738	0.9744	0.9750	0.9756	0.9761	0.9767

(From the Cumulative normal distribution table)

2. The student's *t* distribution table

This distribution is used for small samples where $n < 30$ to obtain critical t values. Read the critical value that corresponds to the level of significance, α, and the degrees of freedom. The degree of freedom for one sample is $n - 1$, and for two samples is $n1 + n2 - 2$. The "n" represents the sample size.

The critical values of the Student t distribution for a sample with 12 degrees of freedom at $\alpha = 0.05$ are 2.179 for a two-tailed test and 1.782 for a one-tailed test. This is illustrated in Figure 9.7 below:

Figure 9.7   The *t* distribution: Critical values of *t*

TABLE A.2

t Distribution: Critical Values of t

Degrees of freedom	Two-tailed test: One-tailed test:	10% 5%	5% 2.5%	2% 1%	1% 0.5%	0.2% 0.1%	0.1% 0.05%
				Significance level			
1		6.314	12.706	31.821	63.657	318.309	636.619
2		2.920	4.303	6.965	9.925	22.327	31.599
3		2.353	3.182	4.541	5.841	10.215	12.924
4		2.132	2.776	3.747	4.604	7.173	8.610
5		2.015	2.571	3.365	4.032	5.893	6.869
6		1.943	2.447	3.143	3.707	5.208	5.959
7		1.894	2.365	2.998	3.499	4.785	5.408
8		1.860	2.306	2.896	3.355	4.501	5.041
9		1.833	2.262	2.821	3.250	4.297	4.781
10		1.812	2.228	2.764	3.169	4.144	4.587
11		1.796	2.201	2.718	3.106	4.025	4.437
12		1.782	2.179	2.681	3.055	3.930	4.318

(From the Critical values of the t distribution table)

3. Chi-square tables

This table is used to test for independence and goodness of fit. It is used when data is categorical.

Read the critical value that corresponds to the degrees of freedom and the level of significance. The degrees of freedom are obtained by (rows- 1) *(columns- 1).

Example: The critical value of the chi-square with 9 degrees of freedom at $\alpha = 0.05$ is 16.919. This is illustrated in Figure 9.8 below:

Figure 9.8 Chi-squared distribution

TABLE A.4

χ^2 (Chi-Squared) Distribution: Critical Values of χ^2

Significance level

Degrees of freedom	5%	1%	0.1%
1	3.841	6.635	10.828
2	5.991	9.210	13.816
3	7.815	11.345	16.266
4	9.488	13.277	18.467
5	11.070	15.086	20.515
6	12.592	16.812	22.458
7	14.067	18.475	24.322
8	15.507	20.090	26.124
9	16.919	21.666	27.877
10	18.307	23.209	29.588

(From Critical values of the chi-squared distribution table)

4. F distribution tables

This table is used with F tests for the ANOVA. Read the critical F value that corresponds to the level of significance, α, and the numerator degrees of freedom ($v1$) and denominator degrees of freedom ($v2$).

Example: The critical F value at $\alpha = 0.05$, 5 numerator degrees of freedom and 5 denominator degrees of freedom is 5.05. This is illustrated in Figure 9.9 below:

| Figure 9.9 | The *F* distribution: Critical values of *F* |

TABLE A.3

F Distribution: Critical Values of *F* (5% significance level)

v_1	1	2	3	4	5	6	7	8	9	10	12	14	16	18	20
v_2															
1	161.45	199.50	215.71	224.58	230.16	233.99	236.77	238.88	240.54	241.88	243.91	245.36	246.46	247.32	248.01
2	18.51	19.00	19.16	19.25	19.30	19.33	19.35	19.37	19.38	19.40	19.41	19.42	19.43	19.44	19.45
3	10.13	9.55	9.28	9.12	9.01	8.94	8.89	8.85	8.81	8.79	8.74	8.71	8.69	8.67	8.66
4	7.71	6.94	6.59	6.39	6.26	6.16	6.09	6.04	6.00	5.96	5.91	5.87	5.84	5.82	5.80
5	6.61	5.79	5.41	5.19	5.05	4.95	4.88	4.82	4.77	4.74	4.68	4.64	4.60	4.58	4.56
6	5.99	5.14	4.76	4.53	4.39	4.28	4.21	4.15	4.10	4.06	4.00	3.96	3.92	3.90	3.87

(From Critical values of the F distribution table)

Another important term to understand in hypothesis testing is p-value, which we will cover in the next section.

9.4.7 P-value

It is the probability of obtaining a value at least equal to or greater than an observation when the null hypothesis is true. The p-value is used together with the significance level. Once a p-value is determined, it is compared against the chosen significance level as discussed in Section 9.4.1, leading to the rejection or failure to reject the null hypothesis. Statistical software provides the p-value for each statistical test performed.

Making the decision in hypothesis testing:

1. The p-value method:

   Reject H_0 if the p-value is less than or equal to α.

   Fail to reject H_0 if the p-value is greater than α.

2. The critical value method:

   Reject H_0 if the test statistic lies in the rejection region.

   Fail to reject H_0 if the test statistic lies in the acceptance region.

9.5 General Procedure of Hypothesis Testing

Before we step into the concluding sections of this book, let's summarize the general steps to test a hypothesis as follows:

1. State the null and alternative hypotheses. Differentiate between what you want to disprove and what should be proved.

2. Set the significance level (α). The $\alpha = 0.05$ or 5% is conventionally used.

3. Collect data that will help you test the hypotheses. The sample should be representative of the true population.

4. Identify the appropriate test statistic and calculate it or determine the p-value. After you've decided on a test, you may use the data from the sample to calculate the test statistic. The p-value, which shows the likelihood of getting the observed data if the null hypothesis is true, can also be directly provided by statistical software.

5. Construct the rejection and acceptance regions that will help make a decision.

6. Draw a conclusion.

9.5.1 Statistical tests and hypothesis testing

Depending on the nature of the data available, any of the statistical tests discussed under this section may be chosen. A statistical test provides information that enables professionals to make appropriate decisions regarding the hypothesis being tested. Many popular tests exist, each tailored to a particular set of data and research problems; these include the Z test, the independent samples t-test, the paired samples t-test, and the chi-square test. If you want your hypothesis tests to be relevant and accurate, you need to learn when to use each one.

1. Z test

The Z test is a statistical test that is used to validate whether means are different from each other or from a hypothesized mean value. This test is used for large samples where n>30 and the variance is known.

A market survey in 2016 concluded that an average American woman spends less than $80 on makeup in a week. A researcher wants to test if this finding holds in 2024. The researcher randomly asked 36 American women how much they spend on makeup in a week. The following data was collected:

60, 70, 75, 55, 80, 55, 50, 40, 45, 80, 70, 50, 95, 120, 90, 75, 85, 90, 80, 60, 110, 65, 80, 85, 85, 45, 70, 75, 60, 90, 90, 60, 95, 110, 85, 70.

The prices are in dollars. Perform a hypothesis test to test the finding at $\alpha = 0.05$.

Solution:

Let's carry out the test as per the steps summarized at the beginning of Section 9.5 above.

Step 1: State the null and alternative hypotheses.

Null hypothesis (H_0): An average American woman spends $80 on make-up in a week($H_0$:$\mu = \$80$).

Alternative hypothesis (H_a): An average American woman spends less than $80 on make-up in a week (H_a: $\mu < 80$).

Step 2: Specify significance level.

The specified significance level is $\alpha = 0.05$.

Step 3: Calculate the test statistic (perform a Z-test).

Start by calculating the mean and the standard deviation: $\bar{x} = 75$, $\sigma = 19.2$ from the data $n = 36$ and from the question $\mu = 80$.

The test statistic, $Z = \dfrac{\bar{x} - \mu}{\dfrac{\sigma}{\sqrt{n}}} = \dfrac{75 - 80}{\dfrac{19.2}{\sqrt{36}}} = -1.56$

Step 4: Construct the rejection and acceptance region.

The specified hypothesis is a one-sided test where the alternative hypothesis points to the left (spending on make-up less than $80). Therefore, the z critical value for a left-tailed test will be read from the normal distribution at $\alpha = 0.05$.

Z critical value for $\alpha = 0.05 = -1.65$. See Figure 9.10 below:

| Figure 9.10 | The normal distribution |

z	0.00	0.01	0.02	0.03	0.04	0.05	0.06	0.07	0.08	0.09
0.0	0.5000	0.5040	0.5080	0.5120	0.5160	0.5199	0.5239	0.5279	0.5319	0.5359
0.1	0.5398	0.5438	0.5478	0.5517	0.5557	0.5596	0.5636	0.5675	0.5714	0.5753
0.2	0.5793	0.5832	0.5871	0.5910	0.5948	0.5987	0.6026	0.6064	0.6103	0.6141
0.3	0.6179	0.6217	0.6255	0.6293	0.6331	0.6368	0.6406	0.6443	0.6480	0.6517
0.4	0.6554	0.6591	0.6628	0.6664	0.6700	0.6736	0.6772	0.6808	0.6844	0.6879
0.5	0.6915	0.6950	0.6985	0.7019	0.7054	0.7088	0.7123	0.7157	0.7190	0.7224
0.6	0.7257	0.7291	0.7324	0.7357	0.7389	0.7422	0.7454	0.7486	0.7517	0.7549
0.7	0.7580	0.7611	0.7642	0.7673	0.7704	0.7734	0.7764	0.7794	0.7823	0.7852
0.8	0.7881	0.7910	0.7939	0.7967	0.7995	0.8023	0.8051	0.8078	0.8106	0.8133
0.9	0.8159	0.8186	0.8212	0.8238	0.8264	0.8289	0.8315	0.8340	0.8365	0.8389
1.0	0.8413	0.8438	0.8461	0.8485	0.8508	0.8531	0.8554	0.8577	0.8599	0.8621
1.1	0.8643	0.8665	0.8686	0.8708	0.8729	0.8749	0.8770	0.8790	0.8810	0.8830
1.2	0.8849	0.8869	0.8888	0.8907	0.8925	0.8944	0.8962	0.8980	0.8997	0.9015
1.3	0.9032	0.9049	0.9066	0.9082	0.9099	0.9115	0.9131	0.9147	0.9162	0.9177
1.4	0.9192	0.9207	0.9222	0.9236	0.9251	0.9265	0.9279	0.9292	0.9306	0.9319
1.5	0.9332	0.9345	0.9357	0.9370	0.9382	0.9394	0.9406	0.9418	0.9429	0.9441
1.6	0.9452	0.9463	0.9474	0.9484	0.9495	0.9505	0.9515	0.9525	0.9535	0.9545
1.7	0.9554	0.9564	0.9573	0.9582	0.9591	0.9599	0.9608	0.9616	0.9625	0.9633

(From the Cumulative normal distribution table)

Please find more details by referring to the "Statistical Tables" section at the end of the book.

Step 5: Conclusion.

The absolute value of the Z test statistic is 1.56, which is less than the absolute value of the Z critical value (1.644854).

The rejection and acceptance of the normal distribution is shown below in Figure 9.11:

Figure 9.11 **The rejection and acceptance of the normal distribution**

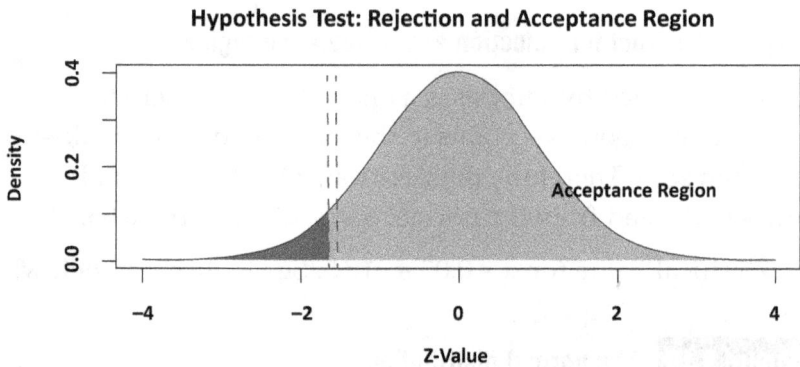

The region highlighted in red is the rejection region.

The Z test value, shown by the purple line, falls in the acceptance region. This means that the null hypothesis is not rejected. The conclusion is that an average American woman spends $80 on makeup in a week.

2. Independent samples t-test

An independent sample t-test analyzes the means for two independent groups.

For example, a restaurant manager wants to know which of his two employees does more work than the other. The manager records the number of guests served by each of the employees over some time, as shown below.

Table 9.1	Number of guests served by each of the employees

Employee A	60 70 75 55 80 55 50 40 45 80 70 50 95 120 90
Employee B	80 60 110 65 80 85 85 45 70 75 60 90 90 60 95

Using this data, is there sufficient evidence to suggest that one employee serves more customers than the other? Use $\alpha = 0.05$.

Solution:

Step 1: State the null and alternative hypotheses.

Null hypothesis (H_0): There is no difference in the number of guests served by the two employees (H_0: $\mu_1 = \mu_2$).

Alternative hypothesis (H_a): There is a difference in the number of guests served by the two employees (H_1: $\mu_1 \neq \mu_2$).

Step 2: Specify significance level.

The specified significance level is $\alpha = 0.05$.

Step 3: Calculate the test statistic by performing an independent sample t-test.

The t-test value can be calculated manually using the formula below:

$$t = \frac{\bar{x}1 - \bar{x}2}{\sqrt{\left(\frac{s1^2}{n1} + \frac{s2^2}{n2} \right)}}$$

Here:
- t = Student's t-test
- $\bar{x}1$ = mean of group 1

- $\bar{x}2$ = mean of group 2
- $s1$ = standard deviation of group 1
- $s2$ = standard deviation of group 2
- $n1$ = number of observations in group 1
- $n2$ = number of observations in group 2

The test can also be performed by statistical software to give the output as shown in Figure 9.12.

Figure 9.12 **Output resulting from using a statistical software**

➔ T-Test

[DataTest]

Group Statistics

	Employee	N	Mean	Std. Deviation	Std. Error Mean
Employee A	A	15	69.0000	21.72885	5.61036
	B	15	76.6667	16.86783	4.35526

Independent Samples Test

		Levene's Test for Equality of Variances		t-test for Equality of Means						
									95% Confidence Interval of the Difference	
		F	Sig.	t	df	Sig. (2-tailed)	Mean Difference	Std. Error Difference	Lower	Upper
Employee A	Equal variances assumed	.747	.395	-1.079	28	.290	-7.66667	7.10243	-22.21533	6.88199
	Equal variances not assumed			-1.079	26.378	.290	-7.66667	7.10243	-22.25573	6.92240

The test value is $t(28) = -1.079$

The critical value can be read from the student's t distribution tables (added under "Statistical Tables" at the end of the book) by checking a value that corresponds to 28 degrees of freedom and $\alpha = 0.05$ which is 2.048 as shown in Figure 9.13 below:

Figure 9.13 Critical value of the t distribution table

16	1.746	2.120	2.583	2.921	3.686	4.015
17	1.740	2.110	2.567	2.898	3.646	3.965
18	1.734	2.101	2.552	2.878	3.610	3.922
19	1.729	2.093	2.539	2.861	3.579	3.883
20	1.725	2.086	2.528	2.845	3.552	3.850
21	1.721	2.080	2.518	2.831	3.527	3.819
22	1.717	2.074	2.508	2.819	3.505	3.792
23	1.714	2.069	2.500	2.807	3.485	3.768
24	1.711	2.064	2.492	2.797	3.467	3.745
25	1.708	2.060	2.485	2.787	3.450	3.725
26	1.706	2.056	2.479	2.779	3.435	3.707
27	1.703	2.052	2.473	2.771	3.421	3.690
28	1.701	2.048	2.467	2.763	3.408	3.674
29	1.699	2.045	2.462	2.756	3.396	3.659

(From the Critical values of the t distribution table)

Step 4: Rejection and acceptance.

The absolute value of the calculated test statistic, 1.079, is less than the critical value. The test value falls in the acceptance region.

Additionally, the p-value generated for the test statistic ($p = 0.290$) is greater than the specified significance level.

Step 5: Conclusion.

The arguments in step 4 above imply that the null hypothesis is not rejected. Therefore, there is no difference in the number of guests served by the two employees.

3. Paired samples t-test

A paired samples t-test is also known as a dependent samples t-test. This test is done for two measurements from the same person, item, or object. It is appropriate for processes that occur at different times, for instance, a company introducing training programs to its employees.

Productivity is measured before and after the employees undergo the training programs. We can compare the mean productivity before and after the training. This will help to determine whether the training impacts productivity.

Under the paired samples t-test, the null and alternative hypotheses for a two-tailed test are stated as follows:

H_0: $\mu_1 = \mu_2$ (the paired population means are equal)

H_1: $\mu_1 \neq \mu_2$ (the paired population means are not equal)

Alternatively,

H_0: $\mu_1 - \mu_2 = 0$ (the difference between the paired population means is equal to zero)

H_1: $\mu_1 - \mu_2 \neq 0$ (the difference between the paired population means is not zero)

μ_1 and μ_2 are the means for variable 1 and variable 2, respectively.

The paired-sample t-test can be calculated using the formula below:

$$t = \frac{\overline{x}_{diff} - 0}{s_{\overline{x}}}$$

Where

$$s_{\overline{x}} = \frac{s_{diff}}{\sqrt{n}}$$

$\overline{x}$ diff = Sample mean of the differences.

n = Sample size.

sdiff = Sample standard deviation of the differences.

$s\overline{x}$ = Estimated standard error of the mean.

The degrees of freedom for the test are given by $df = n - 1$.

Example

Let us proceed with the productivity example above by looking at the real data shown in Figure 9.14 below:

Figure 9.14 (A)   Paired two-sample for means

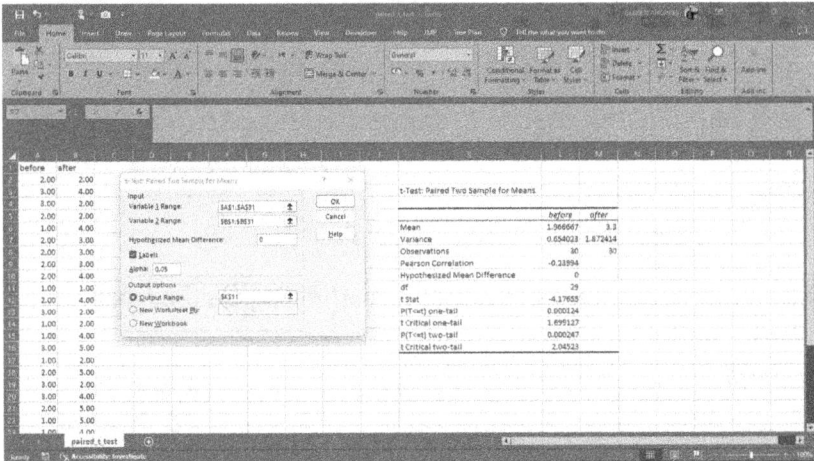

Figure 9.14 (B)   Paired two-sample for means

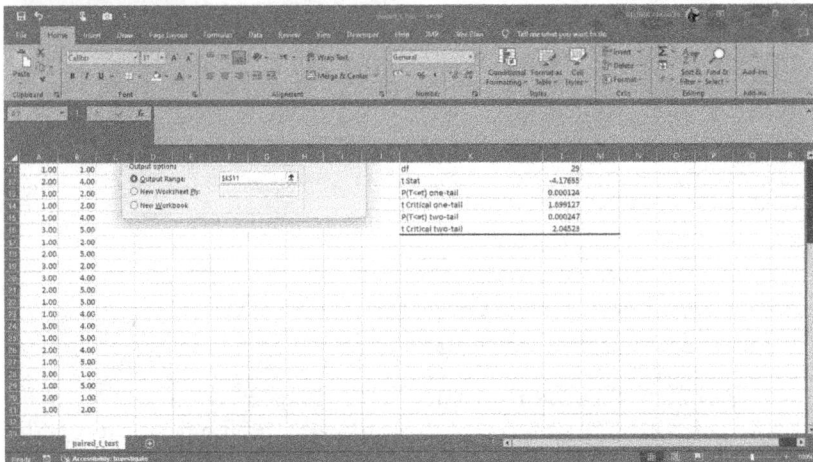

This data shows the productivity of employees before and after training. Does it suggest a difference in the mean productivity before and after training at $\alpha = 0.05$?

Solution:

Step 1: State the null and alternative hypotheses.

H_0: $\mu_1 = \mu_2$ (the paired productivity means are equal)

H_1: $\mu_1 \neq \mu_2$ (the paired productivity means are not equal)

Step 2: Specify significance level.

The specified significance level is $\alpha = 0.05$.

Step 3: Calculate the test statistic by performing a paired samples t-test.

The output generated from Excel is shown below in Figure 9.15.

Figure 9.15 **The output from Excel of the test statistic**

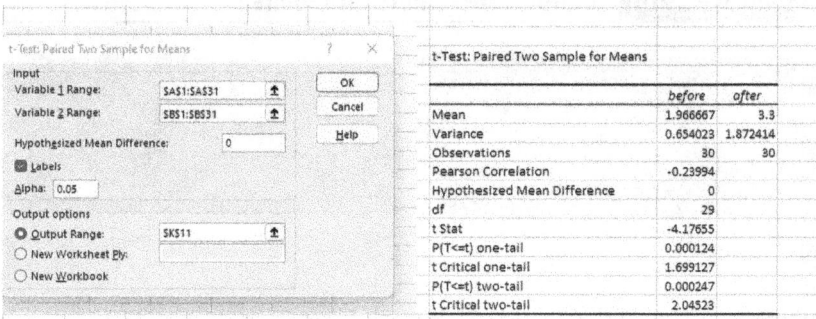

The test value is $t(29) = -4.17655$.

The critical t value that corresponds to 29 degrees of freedom and $\alpha = 0.05$ for a two-tailed test is 2.045, as shown in Figure 9.16 below:

Figure 9.16	The *t* Distribution: Critical values of *t*

16	1.746	2.120	2.583	2.921	3.686	4.015
17	1.740	2.110	2.567	2.898	3.646	3.965
18	1.734	2.101	2.552	2.878	3.610	3.922
19	1.729	2.093	2.539	2.861	3.579	3.883
20	1.725	2.086	2.528	2.845	3.552	3.850
21	1.721	2.080	2.518	2.831	3.527	3.819
22	1.717	2.074	2.508	2.819	3.505	3.792
23	1.714	2.069	2.500	2.807	3.485	3.768
24	1.711	2.064	2.492	2.797	3.467	3.745
25	1.708	2.060	2.485	2.787	3.450	3.725
26	1.706	2.056	2.479	2.779	3.435	3.707
27	1.703	2.052	2.473	2.771	3.421	3.690
28	1.701	2.048	2.467	2.763	3.408	3.674
29	1.699	2.045	2.462	2.756	3.396	3.659

(From the Critical values of the t distribution table)

Step 4: Rejection and acceptance.

The absolute value of the calculated test statistic, 4.17655, is greater than the critical value, 2.04523. The test value falls within the rejection region.

Additionally, the p-value generated for the test statistic (p = 0.000247) is less than the significance level specified.

Step 5: Conclusion.

The arguments in step 4 above imply that the null hypothesis is rejected. The paired productivity means are not equal. There is a difference in the mean productivity before and after the training.

4. Chi-square test

A chi-square test is useful when the data is organized in a contingency table. The test can be used to check for independence between categorical variables and also to test for goodness of fit.

The formula used to calculate the chi-square test statistic is:

$$\chi^2 = \sum \frac{(O_i - E_i)^2}{E_i}$$

χ^2 = chi squared

O_i = observed value

E_i = expected value

For example, a media house conducts a survey to determine whether there is a relationship between television programs watched by male and female genders. The following data is collected from a random survey of 810 people.

Table 9.2 **The type of program watched by both genders**

Program	Gender	
	Male	Female
News	170	160
Movies	130	120
Sports	150	80

Does the data provide sufficient evidence to suggest that a television program and gender are related at $\alpha = 0.05$?

Step 1: State the null and alternative hypotheses.

H_0: The type of television program and the gender are independent (the gender does not determine what someone watches on TV).

H_1: The type of television program and the gender are dependent (the gender determines what someone watches on TV).

Step 2: Specify significance level.

The specified significance level is $\alpha = 0.05$

Step 3: Calculate the test statistic by performing a chi-square test.

The chi-square test can be performed in Excel using either CHISQ.TEST or CHITEST function. The output generated from the Excel worksheet is shown below in Figure 9.17.

Figure 9.17 The output of the chi-square test

chi square test statistic	12.15747
degrees of freedom	2
p-value	0.002291

The chi-square test statistic is $\chi 2(2) = 12.15747$ with a p-value = 0.002291.

The critical chi-square value with 2 degrees of freedom at $\alpha = 0.05$ is $\chi 2(2) = 5.991$ as shown in Figure 9.18 below:

> Please find more details by referring to the "Statistical Tables" section at the end of the book.

Figure 9.18 Critical values of the chi-squared distribution

TABLE A.4

χ^2 (Chi-Squared) Distribution: Critical Values of χ^2

Significance level

Degrees of freedom	5%	1%	0.1%
1	3.841	6.635	10.828
2	5.991	9.210	13.816
3	7.815	11.345	16.266
4	9.488	13.277	18.467
5	11.070	15.086	20.515
6	12.592	16.812	22.458
7	14.067	18.475	24.322
8	15.507	20.090	26.124

(From Critical values of the chi-squared distribution table)

Step 4: Rejection and acceptance.

The calculated chi-square test value is greater than the critical chi-square value. The null hypothesis is rejected.

Step 5: Conclusion.

The type of television program and the gender are dependent. There is a significant relationship between the television program and a person's gender.

By completing this section, we have reached the end of the chapter, marking the end of the book. We have been through a comprehensive journey through the key concepts and methods of business statistics, equipping you with the tools necessary to analyze data, draw meaningful conclusions, and make informed decisions.

In the first half of the book, we saw what business statistics entails, and how to collect, present, and summarize the organized data using statistical tools. Further, we saw that statisticians don't use data from the whole population but rather sample it for analysis using the various sampling techniques discussed in this book.

The second half of this book introduced you to inferential statistics, i.e., probability, sampling, regression, correlation, and finally, hypothesis testing. Understanding these topics equips enterprises and professionals with skills such as organizing and interpreting data, exploring variability and relationships between variables, assessing probabilities, and making predictions.

Hypothesis testing, discussed in this last chapter, is the final step for a statistician or data analyst. This is because the end of any research problem must end with a decision. This decision must be made from testing a hypothesis about the data.

Chapter Summary

- Hypothesis testing is the process of testing the assumptions, propositions, or claims about population parameters by collecting data from a sample and analyzing and drawing conclusions based on the results.

- A hypothesis starts by specifying the null and the alternative hypotheses. The null hypothesis is a claim that should be disproved, while the alternative hypothesis is what the researcher needs to prove.

- Two types of errors could arise from testing a hypothesis: type I and type II errors. A Type I error occurs when the investigator or researcher rejects a null hypothesis when it is true. It is also known as a "false positive" conclusion. A type II error, also known as a false negative, is the decision to fail to reject the null hypothesis when it is false.

- A hypothesis may be tested using the p-value method and the test statistic method (traditional method).

- A hypothesis may originate from multiple sources, including theories, benchmarks, and trends in the industry, or from popular beliefs.

- A critical region, commonly referred to as the rejection region, is the region that contains all the values of the test statistic that lead to the rejection of the null hypothesis.

- There are many statistical tests, including the Z test, the independent samples t-test, the paired samples t-test, and the chi-square test. Depending on the research question and the specified hypotheses, an appropriate test must be chosen.

Further Learning

(Links also available in Online Resources)

1. **Choosing a statistical test**
   http://bit.ly/3HgEm9C

2. **Different types of statistical tests explained**
   http://bit.ly/4oGTiP5

3. **Hypothesis Testing**
   http://bit.ly/4mgYlUE

Quiz

1. **What is hypothesis testing?**

    a. Construction of the rejection and acceptance region to help determine whether a claim or proposition is true

    b. The process of testing the assumptions, propositions, or claims about population parameters by collecting data from a sample, analyzing it, and drawing conclusions based on the results

    c. Calculating the test statistic that can be used to determine whether a claim or proposition is true

2. **The following are the steps used in testing a hypothesis:**

    i. State the null and alternative hypotheses.

    ii. Collect data that will help you test the hypotheses.

    iii. Identify the correct test statistic.

    iv. Set the significance level.

    v. Construct the rejection and acceptance regions.

    vi. Draw a conclusion.

    Arrange them in the correct sequence.

    a. i, iii, ii, v, iv, vi

    b. i, iv, iii, v, ii, vi

    c. i, iv, ii, iii, v, vi

3. **Differentiate between Type I and Type II errors in hypothesis testing.**

   a. A Type I error occurs when the researcher fails to reject the null hypothesis when it is false, while a Type II error occurs when the null hypothesis is true but rejected.

   b. A Type I error occurs when the researcher rejects a null hypothesis when it is true, while a Type II error is the decision to fail to reject the null hypothesis when it is false.

   c. A Type I error occurs when the alternative hypothesis is not accepted when it is true, while a Type II error occurs when the null hypothesis is true but rejected.

4. **All the following may give rise to a testable hypothesis except?**

   a. Popular beliefs
   b. Unfalsifiable statements
   c. Industry trends and benchmarks

5. **Which of the following statements is true about significance level?**

   a. It is the risk or probability of rejecting the null hypothesis when it is true.

   b. It is the probability of failing to reject the null hypothesis when it is false.

   c. It is the probability that no Type I or Type II error will be committed in a hypothesis test.

6. **What is a confidence interval?**

   a. It is an interval that contains all the decisions likely to favor a researcher's hypothesis.

   b. It is the interval within which estimates are expected to fall when the analysis is done with a certain confidence.

   c. It is an interval that contains all the probabilities that support the null hypothesis.

7. **Calculate the confidence level if a significance level is set at 0.10.**

   a. 0.95

   b. 0.80

   c. 0.90

8. **A shoe factory has been recording shoe sales for each day of the month starting from January to December. During the yearly review in December 2024, it was noted that the average daily shoe sale for the year was 65 with a standard deviation of 9. During the half-year review in June, the factory board raised concerns that this year's average daily shoe sales could be below the previous year's.**

   The quality department wants to investigate the claim. A random sample of 35 days is selected and the average daily sale is found to be 61.5.
   Test the claim at a 5% level of significance. (Detailed solution included in Online Resources.)

a. There is no sufficient evidence to conclude that the average daily sale in the current year could fall below 65.

b. There is sufficient evidence to conclude that the average daily sale in the current year could fall below 65.

c. The available information is not sufficient to conclude.

9. **In the context of question 8 above, what is a Type I error?**

a. Concluding that the average daily sale is above 65 when that is false

b. Concluding that the average daily sale is below 65 when it is not

c. Concluding that the average daily sale is exactly 65 when that is false

10. **A supermarket attendant believes that gender (male or female) has a relationship with a customer's shopping method (in-store, online). The attendant collects data on the counts of a customer's gender and the shipping method they use. In testing the hypothesis, why is the chi-square method preferred?**

a. The data collected is categorical.

b. The data collected is continuous.

c. The sample size is likely less than 30.

Answers

1 – b	2 – c	3 – b	4 – b	5 – a
6 – b	7 – c	8 – b	9 – b	10 – a

Inventory Management Optimization Using Business Statistics

Overview:

StatEdge Electronics is an electronics retail business based in Cleveland, dealing with accessories such as smartphones, tablets, TV sets, and CCTV cameras. Over the past six months, StatEdge Electronics has experienced stocking challenges where highly in-demand products stock out faster, while less-demand accessories are overstocked. These challenges have led to the loss of sales for in-demand accessories and more costs resulting from overstocking less-demand goods.

To this effect, the central management of StatEdge Electronics has directed the operations team to find ways to address the challenges identified. The goal is to ensure that in-demand accessories are overstocked to meet demand while unnecessary stocking costs are cut by stocking lower quantities of less-demand accessories. The operations team settled on business statistics techniques and tools, such as inventory forecasting and optimization, for better decision-making on stocking.

Business situation:

- **Stockouts:** In-demand accessories like the latest smartphone models often went out of stock quickly. This resulted in missed sales.
- **Overstocking:** Less-demand accessories tended to stay in inventory for months, leading to high storage costs and wasted resources.
- **Inventory turnover:** StatEdge Electronics struggled to balance inventory turnover rates across different product lines.

Key questions:

- How can StatEdge Electronics predict future demand for in-demand accessories and prevent stockouts?
- How can the company minimize overstocking of less-demand accessories and maintain adequate inventory levels?
- What statistical techniques are most appropriate for demand forecasting in this context?

Approach:

To address the above challenges, the operations team uses historical sales data. This includes monthly sales volumes, demand fluctuations, and seasonal trends. By employing statistical tools like time series forecasting and regression analysis, they develop an inventory optimization model. For this purpose, they also rely on moving averages, which smooth out fluctuations by calculating the means over time.

Further, the team applies descriptive statistics to analyze the mean sales volumes for each product category and identify high-demand and low-demand products. Regression analysis is used to predict the impact of external variables such as holidays or promotional events on product sales. Additionally, probability distribution models are used to estimate the likelihood of stockouts and excess inventory based on current stock levels.

Case assignment:

1. Using the historical sales data, calculate the monthly average sales volume for each product line.
2. Apply time series forecasting to predict future demand for the next three months. What trends do you observe in the data?
3. Use regression analysis to identify which external factors (holidays, promotional periods) have the most significant impact on sales volume.
4. Propose an inventory optimization plan based on the insights gained from your statistical analysis.

Detailed solution:

The key solutions and learnings on how StatEdge Electronics addressed its inventory management challenges and optimized stock levels are as follows:

1. Predicting future demand using time series forecasting:

StatEdge Electronics performs a time series analysis that involves analyzing a sequence of data points collected or recorded at regular time intervals. This analysis reveals various cycles and patterns. By detecting seasonal trends such as increased smartphone sales during holiday seasons, StatEdge Electronics can adjust its stock proactively. This accurate demand forecasting helps prevent stockouts, ensuring the supply of high-demand products.

2. Reducing overstocking with descriptive and probability analysis:

StatEdge Electronics analyzes mean sales volumes for each product line to distinguish between high-demand and low-demand accessories. Appropriate probability distribution models are used to estimate the likelihood of excess inventory. Based on such data-driven insights, the company minimizes overstocking. It sets optimal reorder points by relying on demand probability, reducing storage costs and waste.

3. Identifying external demand drivers with regression analysis:

The company performs a regression analysis to determine the influence of external factors, such as holidays, promotions, and economic conditions, on sales volume. Regression analysis is expected to identify promotional campaigns that significantly increase demand. Thus, it justifies the need for pre-event inventory boosts. StatEdge Electronics' understanding of external factors helps in strategic planning, ensuring stock levels align with anticipated fluctuations.

4. Developing an inventory optimization plan:

The insights from statistical analyses help the company draft an inventory plan that includes dynamic stocking strategies and adjustments of stock levels based on forecasted demand. The company also automates restocking alerts, triggered when inventory levels drop below critical thresholds. Finally, the company segments stocking, where high-turnover items are prioritized for quick replenishment. Thus, StatEdge Electronics's data-driven inventory management system improves efficiency, balancing demand fulfillment with cost control.

Customer Segmentation and Targeted Marketing Using Business Statistics

Overview:

LifeStat is a renowned seller of health-tracking wearable devices such as posture detectors, continuous glucose monitors, and wearable defibrillators. The company wants to make sure that its products reach only those customers needing specified wearable devices. To achieve the objective, the company thinks that segmentation of its customer base into distinct groups will help in reaching out to each group with personalized devices. The company hires the services of a business analyst who has promised to use statistical tools to analyze customer data and develop a data-driven targeted marketing campaign.

Business situation:

- **Customer base:** The business analyst has accumulated significant customer data from LifeStat. This includes purchase history, demographic information, and usage patterns of their wearables.

- **Marketing challenge:** The company's current marketing approach is generic and not tailored to specific customer needs. This results in low conversion rates for marketing campaigns.
- **Goal:** The objective is to segment the customer base and target specific groups with personalized offers, thereby improving the effectiveness of marketing campaigns and increasing sales.

Key questions:

- What are the key customer segments that LifeStat should focus on, based on the statistical analysis?
- How can LifeStat use insights from the data to tailor marketing messages to different customer segments?
- What impact does targeted marketing have on customer retention and overall sales?

Approach:

The hired business analyst starts by gathering relevant data from multiple sources, including customer purchases, website activity, and customer feedback. Cluster analysis, a statistical technique, is used to segment customers based on shared characteristics, such as age, income level, purchase frequency, and product preferences.

The business analyst is of the view that employing descriptive statistics will be vital for segmenting the customers. Thus, the calculation of average spending, product preferences, and geographic location will be done. Additionally, regression analysis will examine the correlation between factors like age and fitness activity with purchasing behavior.

Case assignment:

1. Using the provided customer data, perform cluster analysis to identify three distinct customer segments.

2. For each segment, calculate the average purchase amount and product preferences using descriptive statistics.

3. Conduct a regression analysis to explore the relationship between age, income, and purchasing behavior.

4. Design a targeted marketing campaign for each customer segment based on the insights gained from the statistical analyses.

Detailed solution:

LifeStat's goal was to improve its marketing efficiency by segmenting customers based on shared characteristics and creating personalized marketing campaigns. The company applies the following statistical techniques to analyze customer data and develop targeted strategies.

1. Identifying key customer segments using cluster analysis:

LifeStat's analytical teams identify clusters that help segment customers into three distinct groups based on age, income level, purchase frequency, and product preferences. The segmentation reveals patterns such as younger customers preferring fitness-oriented wearables, while older customers prioritize health-monitoring devices. This allows the business to understand different buyer personas and tailor marketing efforts to their specific needs.

2. Understanding customer behavior using descriptive statistics:

The average purchase amounts, preferred products, and geographic locations are analyzed to gain deeper insights into spending behavior. The analysis is expected to show whether high-income customers tend to purchase premium health devices, while price-sensitive customers prefer budget-friendly options. Thus, running descriptive statistics enables profiling customer groups, leading to better pricing and product placement strategies.

3. Exploring purchase drivers through regression analysis:

Regression analysis helps predict customer preferences, enabling businesses to adjust product offerings accordingly. In this scenario, the application of regression techniques helps determine how factors like age and fitness activity levels influence purchasing decisions. The findings show the correlation between age and demand for medical wearables, and whether fitness-oriented wearables are more popular among younger customers with active lifestyles.

4. Designing a data-driven targeted marketing strategy:

Based on the insights gained, LifeStat can develop personalized marketing campaigns for each segment, which include:

A. Young fitness enthusiasts: Social media campaigns promoting fitness wearables with discount offers.

B. Middle-aged professionals: Email campaigns featuring wellness-focused wearables with productivity benefits.

C. Older health-conscious customers: Direct mail and healthcare partnerships emphasizing medical monitoring devices.

In this way, targeted marketing improves customer engagement, increases conversion rates, and boosts sales.

Statistical Tables

1. **Cumulative normal distribution (Table A.1)**
   https://home.ubalt.edu/ntsbarsh/business-stat/StatistialTables.pdf

2. **Critical values of the t distribution (Table A.2)**
   https://home.ubalt.edu/ntsbarsh/business-stat/StatistialTables.pdf

3. **Critical values of the F distribution (Table A.3)**
   https://home.ubalt.edu/ntsbarsh/business-stat/StatistialTables.pdf

4. **Critical values of the chi-squared distribution (Table A.4)**
   https://home.ubalt.edu/ntsbarsh/business-stat/StatistialTables.pdf

5. **Binomial Probability Distribution Calculator**
   http://bit.ly/46XhmXw

6. **Statistical Tables PDF**
   http://bit.ly/47xLede

References

Clarke, O. (2007, January 31). *Colgate's '80% of dentists recommend' claim under fire.* Marketing Law. https://marketinglaw.osborneclarke.com/retailing/colgates-80-of-dentists-recommend-claim-under-fire/

Bibliography and Suggested Readings

- Black, K. (2019). *Business statistics: For contemporary decision making* (9th ed.). Wiley.

- Bowerman, B. L., Drougas, A. M., & Duckworth, W. M. (2019). *Business statistics and analytics in practice*. McGraw-Hill Education. https://researchworks.creighton.edu/esploro/outputs/991005971873202656

- Newbold, P., Carlson, W. L., & Thorne, B. (2019). *Statistics for business and economics* (9th ed.). Pearson Education. http://ndl.ethernet.edu.et/bitstream/123456789/13768/1/1-Paul%20Newbold.pdf

- Levine, D. M. (2008). *Business statistics: A first course*. Pearson Education India.

- Witte, R. S. (1980). *Statistics*. Holt, Rinehart and Winston.

www.ingramcontent.com/pod-product-compliance
Lightning Source LLC
Chambersburg PA
CBHW050339270326
41926CB00016B/3531